Jesus Calling

(Peace be upon him)

Preface

In the Name of Allah, Most Gracious, Most Merciful

All praise and thanks are due to Allah, the Lord of the Worlds, and peace and blessings be upon our Prophet Muhammad, his kith and kin, his Companions and all those who follow in their footsteps until the Day of Judgment. Whosoever Allah guides will never be led astray, and whosoever He leads astray will never find guidance.

The personality of Jesus (peace be upon him) has been a subject of disagreement and controversy between Islam and Christianity. While Christians consider Jesus a son of God or God, Muslims believe that he is a mere Prophet of Allah whose mission was to confirm the Torah revealed before him, call to monotheism and give glad tidings of the coming of Prophet Muhammad after him. It was this difference over the personality of Jesus that has kept the followers of the two religions apart.

It is an article of Muslims' creed to repose faith in all Prophets of Allah as well as the Divine Scriptures revealed to them. Muslims have been commanded to revere all Prophets with no distinction. In the words of the Glorious Qur'an,

ءَامَنَ ٱلرَّسُولُ بِمَآ أُنزِلَ إِلَيْهِ مِن رَّبِّهِۦ وَٱلْمُؤْمِنُونَ كُلٌّ ءَامَنَ بِٱللَّهِ وَمَلَٰٓئِكَتِهِۦ وَكُتُبِهِۦ وَرُسُلِهِۦ لَا نُفَرِّقُ بَيْنَ أَحَدٍ مِّن رُّسُلِهِۦ وَقَالُوا۟ سَمِعْنَا وَأَطَعْنَا غُفْرَانَكَ رَبَّنَا وَإِلَيْكَ ٱلْمَصِيرُ ﴿٢٨٥﴾ ﴾ [البقرة: ٢٨٥]

"The Messenger believeth in what hath been revealed to him from his Lord, as do the men of faith, each one (of them) believeth in Allah, His angels, His Books, and His Messengers. "We make no distinction (they say) between one and another of His Messengers."

(Al-Baqarah: 285)

Thus, Muslims hold all Prophets of Allah in high esteem and place them on an equal footing. A Muslim believes in Jesus as he or she believes in Muhammad (peace be upon both of them). In addition to this, a Muslim who disbelieves in any of Allah's Prophets is deemed a disbeliever, according to the Qur'an and Sunnah of Prophet Muhammad, and is supposed to be killed in a state where Islamic law is applied. Even a mere attempt to impeach or accuse Jesus (peace be upon him) of committing a sin is regarded as an act of disbelief, because Muslims believe that all Prophets of Allah are infallible and not liable to sin.

This is not a lip service, it is the dictate of the Qur'an and Sunnah. Our love of Jesus (peace be upon him) knows no bounds, and our feelings towards him run so deep that we give our children the names of Jesus and Mary.

However, Muslims do believe that Allah Almighty is far and above having a child or a partner in His divinity, and therefore they reject any belief that over-exalts Jesus above what Allah Almighty wants him to be.

The Islamic View of Jesus aims at presenting a true

picture of Jesus in Islam, and shows how Christians deviated from his teachings. The book also throws light on the beliefs that Muslims associate with Jesus, such as his Virgin Birth, being able to speak in the cradle, performing miracles, and the descent of Jesus before the end of the world.

The Birth of Jesus
(peace be upon him)

Ibn Katheer states: He is Jesus, the son of Mary. He is Allah's bondman and Messenger. In the beginning of *Surah* (a chapter of the Qur'an) Ali `Imraan, Allah, Exalted be He, revealed eighty three verses to refute the claims of Christians who called Jesus the son of Allah, far be Allah from all these claims. Ibn Katheer goes on to say that a Christian delegation from Najraan came to Prophet Muhammad, peace and blessings be upon him. They mentioned that they believe in the Trinity and claimed that Allah is one of three; the Divine Being, Jesus, and Mary. Then Allah, Exalted be He, revealed the beginning of *Surah* Ali-`Imraan pointing out that Jesus is but a servant of Allah whom He created and fashioned in a womb as He did with other creatures; He created him without a human father just as Adam was born without either a human father or mother. Rather Allah just said be and he was. Allah also explains the birth of Jesus' mother, Mary and how she became pregnant with him, a story which was elucidated in *Surah* Maryam.

The Birth of Mary, Peace Be Upon Her:

Allah Almighty says:

﴿إِنَّ ٱللَّهَ ٱصْطَفَىٰ ءَادَمَ وَنُوحًا وَءَالَ إِبْرَٰهِيمَ وَءَالَ
عِمْرَٰنَ عَلَى ٱلْعَٰلَمِينَ ﴿٣٣﴾ ذُرِّيَّةً بَعْضُهَا مِنۢ بَعْضٍ ۗ وَٱللَّهُ
سَمِيعٌ عَلِيمٌ ﴿٣٤﴾ إِذْ قَالَتِ ٱمْرَأَتُ عِمْرَٰنَ رَبِّ إِنِّي نَذَرْتُ
لَكَ مَا فِى بَطْنِى مُحَرَّرًا فَتَقَبَّلْ مِنِّىٓ ۖ إِنَّكَ أَنتَ ٱلسَّمِيعُ

ٱلْعَلِيمُ ﴿٣٥﴾ فَلَمَّا وَضَعَتْهَا قَالَتْ رَبِّ إِنِّي وَضَعْتُهَا أُنثَىٰ
وَٱللَّهُ أَعْلَمُ بِمَا وَضَعَتْ وَلَيْسَ ٱلذَّكَرُ كَٱلْأُنثَىٰ وَإِنِّي
سَمَّيْتُهَا مَرْيَمَ وَإِنِّي أُعِيذُهَا بِكَ وَذُرِّيَّتَهَا مِنَ ٱلشَّيْطَٰنِ
ٱلرَّجِيمِ ﴿٣٦﴾ فَتَقَبَّلَهَا رَبُّهَا بِقَبُولٍ حَسَنٍ وَأَنبَتَهَا نَبَاتًا
حَسَنًا وَكَفَّلَهَا زَكَرِيَّا كُلَّمَا دَخَلَ عَلَيْهَا زَكَرِيَّا ٱلْمِحْرَابَ
وَجَدَ عِندَهَا رِزْقًا قَالَ يَٰمَرْيَمُ أَنَّىٰ لَكِ هَٰذَا قَالَتْ هُوَ
مِنْ عِندِ ٱللَّهِ إِنَّ ٱللَّهَ يَرْزُقُ مَن يَشَاءُ بِغَيْرِ حِسَابٍ
﴿٣٧﴾ [آل عمران: ٣٣ ـ ٣٧]

"Allah did choose Adam and Noah, the
family of Abraham, and the family of 'Imran
above all people, Offspring, one of the other:
And Allah hearth and knoweth all things.
Behold! a woman of 'Imran said, " O my
Lord! I do dedicate unto Thee what is in my
womb for Thy special service: so accept this
of me: for Thou hearest and knowest all
things." When she was delivered, she said:
'O my Lord! Behold! I am delivered of a
female child!"-And Allah knew best what she
brought forth- "and is no wise the male like
the female. I have named her Mary, and I
commend her and her offspring to Thy
protection from Evil One, the Rejected."
Right graciously did her Lord accept her: He
made her grow in purity and beauty: To the

care of Zakariyyah was she assigned. Every
time that he entered (her) chamber to see
her, he found her supplied with sustenance.
He said," O Mary! Where (comes) this to
you?" She said," From Allah: For Allah
provides sustenance to whom He pleases,
without measure. "

(Ali `Imraan: 33-37)

Allah had chosen Adam, peace be upon
him; He created him Himself, breathed into him of His
spirit, ordered His angles to prostrate themselves before
him, taught him the names of all things, made him dwell
in paradise, and then caused him to come down to earth
for a certain reason which no one knows but Allah. He
also chose Noah (Nooh), peace be upon him, and made
him the first Prophet sent to mankind. He sent him when
people worshipped idols and ascribed many associates
with Allah in His divinity. As Noah tarried a long time
calling his people day and night, openly and secretly, but
his call only caused them to grow more repugnant, he
prayed to Allah so that He might punish them. As a
result, Allah drowned them, save those who followed
Noah, peace be upon him. Likewise, Allah chose the
family of Abraham from whom descended the children of
Ismael and the most honored and the seal of Prophets,
Muhammad, peace and blessings be upon him. Allah,
moreover, chose the family of 'Imran, the father of Mary,
the mother of Jesus, peace be upon him. There is no
disagreement over the fact that Mary is a descendant of
David, peace be upon him. Her father Imraan was the
leader of prayer among the Israelites during his time. Her
mother, Hannah bint (daughter of) Faqood, was a devout

worshipper. Zechariah, according to the majority of scholars was the Prophet of that time. He was the husband of Isaiah (Ashiaa`), sister of Mary. Some other scholars maintain that Zechariah was a husband of Isaiah's maternal aunt, Allah knows best.

Almighty Allah says:

إِذْ قَالَتِ ٱمْرَأَتُ عِمْرَانَ رَبِّ إِنِّى نَذَرْتُ لَكَ مَا فِى بَطْنِى مُحَرَّرًا فَتَقَبَّلْ مِنِّىٓ إِنَّكَ أَنتَ ٱلسَّمِيعُ ٱلْعَلِيمُ ﴿٣٥﴾

[آل عمران: ٣٥]

"Behold! A woman of 'Imran said, "O my Lord! I do dedicate unto Thee what is in my womb for Thy special service: so accept this of me: for Thou hearest and knowest all things."

(Ali `Imraan: 35)

Muhammad Ibn Is-haaq and others state: Mary's mother was barren. One day she saw a bird feeding its young baby, and consequently, felt eager to beget children. So she vowed that if she became pregnant, she would devote her baby to Allah; to be a bondwoman of the Al-Aqsa Mosque (in Jerusalem). She immediately menstruated, and when she became clean, her husband had intercourse with her and Mary, peace be upon her was conceived.

Almighty Allah says: *"When she was delivered, she said: 'O my Lord! Behold! I am delivered of a female child!"-And Allah knew best what she brought forth- and is no wise the male like the female."* Ibn

Katheer explains: From the viewpoint of physical strength and the service of Al-Aqsa Mosque, it was said that people at that time were in the habit of devoting their children as servants to Al-Aqsa Mosque. The wife of Imraan said, *"I have named her Mary."* Scholars consider this verse an evidence on the lawfulness of naming one's baby on the birthday; this is a ruling which was stipulated in the laws preceding Islam and was retained by Islamic Shari'ah. Al-Bukhari mentioned that a man said to the Prophet," O Messenger of Allah! My wife has begotten a baby, what name do you order me to call him?" "Name him Abdur Rahmaan," said the Prophet. It was also mentioned in the two *Sahihs* that Anas Ibn Malik, may Allah be pleased with him, took his brother upon his birth to the Messenger of Allah, peace and blessings be upon him, and the Prophet named him `Abdullaah.

Ibn Katheer states: Ahmad, and At-Tirmidhi and others narrated on the authority of Samura Ibn Jundub that the Prophet, peace and blessings be upon him, said,

"Every new-born child should be greeted on the 7th day after his birth with a welcoming feast, should be given name and has his/her hair should be shaved."

The wife of Imraan said, *"And I commend her and her offspring to Thy protection from Evil One, the Rejected."* This means she took refuge in Allah from the evils of Satan and sought Allah's protection for her child, Jesus, peace be upon him. Allah then answered her call; as it is reported on the authority of Abu Hurairah, may Allah be pleased with him, that the Prophet, peace and blessings be upon him, said,

"Whenever a child is born, Satan touches it. A child, therefore, cries loudly at the time of birth because of the touch of Satan, except Mary and her child." Then Abu Hurairah said, " Recite, if you wish, Allah's saying," And I seek refuge in Thee for her and for her offspring from the outcast Satan." Allah says," Right graciously did her Lord accept her: He made her grow in purity and beauty: To the care of Zechariah."

Exegetes of the Qur'an mention that her mother wrapped her in clothes upon her birth and went to the mosque and gave her to the worshippers. It is most likely that she gave her to them after her weaning period. Being a daughter of their Imam, they vied which of them would be honored with being her guardian. They drew lots, and it was decided in Zechariah's favor. He was the Prophet at that time. Then Mary was raised under Zechariah's wing. Allah says in another verse,

$$﴿ذَٰلِكَ مِنْ أَنبَاءِ ٱلْغَيْبِ نُوحِيهِ إِلَيْكَ ۚ وَمَا كُنتَ لَدَيْهِمْ إِذْ يُلْقُونَ أَقْلَٰمَهُمْ أَيُّهُمْ يَكْفُلُ مَرْيَمَ وَمَا كُنتَ لَدَيْهِمْ إِذْ يَخْتَصِمُونَ ﴾$$

[آل عمران: ٤٤]

" This is part of the tidings of the things unseen, which We reveal unto thee (O Prophet) by inspiration: thou wast not with them when they cast lots with arrows, as to which of them should be charged with the care of Mary: nor wast thou with them when they disputed (the point)."

(Ali 'Imraan: 44)

Ibn Katheer mentions: Everyone drew his pen and a young boy was ordered to choose the lot. Then the boy selected a pen which was Zechariah's. They asked for another lot in which they would throw their pens in water and the pen which would swim against the tide was to be considered the winner. Upon throwing their pens, Zechariah's pen swam against the tide, but they asked for a third lot in which they would throw their pens in the river and the one which would swim with the tide was to be regarded as a winner. They did so, and it was decided in Zechariah's favor. So Zechariah was charged with the care of Mary.

Zechariah then allocated for her a certain place for worship and allowed no one to enter that place except himself. There, Mary used to worship Allah day and night. She took part in the mosque service. She continued to do so until she became the exemplar of piety amongst the Israelites. She was renowned for her unique qualities and good morals. Whenever Zechariah entered her chamber of worship, he found that she had out-of-season fruit. Allah, in this respect, says: "

﴿فَتَقَبَّلَهَا رَبُّهَا بِقَبُولٍ حَسَنٍ وَأَنبَتَهَا نَبَاتًا حَسَنًا وَكَفَّلَهَا زَكَرِيَّا كُلَّمَا دَخَلَ عَلَيْهَا زَكَرِيَّا الْمِحْرَابَ وَجَدَ عِندَهَا رِزْقًا قَالَ يَمَرْيَمُ أَنَّى لَكِ هَذَا قَالَتْ هُوَ مِنْ عِندِ اللَّهِ إِنَّ اللَّهَ يَرْزُقُ مَن يَشَاءُ بِغَيْرِ حِسَابٍ ٣٧﴾

[آل عمران: ٣٧]

Every time that he entered (her) chamber to see her, he found her supplied with sustenance. He said," O Mary! Whence (comes) this to you?' She said, 'From Allah: For Allah provides sustenance to whom He pleases, without measure.'

(Ali `Imraan: 37)

At that time, Zechariah hoped for a son even if he was gray with years. He said," *O My Lord! Grant unto me from Thee a progeny that is pure, for Thou art He that hearth prayer!"*

Mary Being Chosen by Allah:

Almighty Allah says:

وَإِذْ قَالَتِ ٱلْمَلَٰٓئِكَةُ يَٰمَرْيَمُ إِنَّ ٱللَّهَ ٱصْطَفَىٰكِ وَطَهَّرَكِ وَٱصْطَفَىٰكِ عَلَىٰ نِسَآءِ ٱلْعَٰلَمِينَ ۝ يَٰمَرْيَمُ ٱقْنُتِي لِرَبِّكِ وَٱسْجُدِي وَٱرْكَعِي مَعَ ٱلرَّٰكِعِينَ ۝ ذَٰلِكَ مِنْ أَنۢبَآءِ ٱلْغَيْبِ نُوحِيهِ إِلَيْكَ وَمَا كُنتَ لَدَيْهِمْ إِذْ يُلْقُونَ أَقْلَٰمَهُمْ أَيُّهُمْ يَكْفُلُ مَرْيَمَ وَمَا كُنتَ لَدَيْهِمْ إِذْ يَخْتَصِمُونَ ۝ إِذْ قَالَتِ ٱلْمَلَٰٓئِكَةُ يَٰمَرْيَمُ إِنَّ ٱللَّهَ يُبَشِّرُكِ بِكَلِمَةٍ مِّنْهُ ٱسْمُهُ ٱلْمَسِيحُ عِيسَى ٱبْنُ مَرْيَمَ وَجِيهًا فِي ٱلدُّنْيَا وَٱلْءَاخِرَةِ وَمِنَ ٱلْمُقَرَّبِينَ ۝ وَيُكَلِّمُ ٱلنَّاسَ فِي ٱلْمَهْدِ وَكَهْلًا وَمِنَ ٱلصَّٰلِحِينَ ۝ قَالَتْ رَبِّ أَنَّىٰ يَكُونُ لِي وَلَدٌ وَلَمْ يَمْسَسْنِي بَشَرٌ قَالَ كَذَٰلِكِ ٱللَّهُ يَخْلُقُ مَا يَشَآءُ إِذَا قَضَىٰٓ أَمْرًا فَإِنَّمَا يَقُولُ لَهُۥ كُن فَيَكُونُ ۝ وَيُعَلِّمُهُ ٱلْكِتَٰبَ وَٱلْحِكْمَةَ

وَالتَّوْرَئةَ وَالْإِنجِيلَ ۝ وَرَسُولًا إِلَىٰ بَنِى إِسْرَٰٓءِيلَ أَنِّى
قَدْ جِئْتُكُم بِـَٔايَةٍ مِّن رَّبِّكُمْ أَنِّى أَخْلُقُ لَكُم مِّنَ
ٱلطِّينِ كَهَيْـَٔةِ ٱلطَّيْرِ فَأَنفُخُ فِيهِ فَيَكُونُ طَيْرًا بِإِذْنِ
ٱللَّهِ وَأُبْرِئُ ٱلْأَكْمَهَ وَٱلْأَبْرَصَ وَأُحْىِ ٱلْمَوْتَىٰ بِإِذْنِ
ٱللَّهِ وَأُنَبِّئُكُم بِمَا تَأْكُلُونَ وَمَا تَدَّخِرُونَ فِى بُيُوتِكُمْ
إِنَّ فِى ذَٰلِكَ لَءَايَةً لَّكُمْ إِن كُنتُم مُّؤْمِنِينَ ۝
وَمُصَدِّقًا لِّمَا بَيْنَ يَدَىَّ مِنَ ٱلتَّوْرَىٰةِ وَلِأُحِلَّ لَكُم
بَعْضَ ٱلَّذِى حُرِّمَ عَلَيْكُمْ وَجِئْتُكُم بِـَٔايَةٍ مِّن رَّبِّكُمْ
فَٱتَّقُوا۟ ٱللَّهَ وَأَطِيعُونِ ۝ إِنَّ ٱللَّهَ رَبِّى وَرَبُّكُمْ فَٱعْبُدُوهُ
هَٰذَا صِرَٰطٌ مُّسْتَقِيمٌ ۝ ﴿ [آل عمران: ٤٢ ـ ٥١]

" Behold! The angles said, " O Mary! Allah
hath chosen thee and purified thee – chosen
thee above the women of all nations.   O
Mary! Worship thy lord devoutly: prostrate
thyself, and bow down (in prayer) with those
who bow down. This is part of the tidings of
the things unseen, which we reveal unto thee
(O Prophet!) by inspiration : thou wast not
with them when they cast lots with arrows, as
to which of them should be charged with the
care of Mary: nor wast thou with them when
they disputed (the poi nt.) Behold! The angel
said: 'O Mary! Allah giveth thee glad tidings
of a word from him: his name will be Christ
Jesus. The son of Mary, held in honor in this

world and the Hereafter and of (the company of) those nearest to Allah; he shall speak to the people in childhood and in maturity and he shall be (of the company of) of the righteous.' She said, ' O my lord! How shall I have as son when no man hath touched me?' He said, 'Even so: Allah createth what he willeth: when He hath decreed a Plan, He but saith to it "Be" and it is! And Allah will teach him the Book and Wisdom, the Law and the Gospel, and (appoint him) a Messenger to the Children of Israel (with this message): I have come to you, with a Sign from your Lord, in that I make for you out of clay – as it were, the figure a bird, and breathe into it, and it becomes a bird by Allah's leave and I heal those born blind, and the lepers, and I quicken the dead by Allah's leave; and I declare to you what ye eat, and what ye store in your houses. Surely therein is a Sign for you if ye did believe. (I have come to you), to attest the Law which was before me. And to make lawful to you part of what was (before) forbidden to you; I have come to you with a Sign from your Lord. So fear Allah, and obey me." It is Allah who is my Lord and your Lord; then worship Him. This is a way that is straight."

(Ali `Imraan: 42-51)

Ibn Katheer states: Almighty Allah chose Mary from amongst the women of her time; He made her bear a child without a human father, and gave her glad tidings that he would be a Prophet: *"held in honor in this world and the Hereafter and of (the company of) those nearest to Allah "* meaning he will have a dignified status in Allah's sight in this world as he received a message from Allah and in the Hereafter as he will intercede in favor of those Allah allows him to. *"He shall speak to the people in childhood"* i.e., in his infancy. He performed a miracle when he called people to worship Allah and ascribe no partner with him. *"And in maturity "* meaning when he is adult.

Mary, peace be upon her, was ordered by Allah to increase worship, prayer, bowing, and prostration to Him so that she might be qualified for such a bliss, and that she might be grateful to Allah. The angels said to her, *" O Mary! Allah hath chosen thee and purified thee – chosen thee above the women of all nations. "* That is to say Allah selected Mary, cleared her from vices, granted her lofty morals and made her the best woman of all nations. It may also mean that she was made superior to the women of her time, as it was the case with Moses and the children of Israel. Concerning Moses, Allah, Exalted be He, says,

$$﴿قَالَ يَٰمُوسَىٰٓ إِنِّى ٱصۡطَفَيۡتُكَ عَلَى ٱلنَّاسِ بِرِسَٰلَٰتِى وَبِكَلَٰمِى فَخُذۡ مَآ ءَاتَيۡتُكَ وَكُن مِّنَ ٱلشَّٰكِرِينَ ۝﴾$$

[الأعراف: ١٤٤]

" O Moses! I have chosen thee above other men"

(Al 'Ar`aaf: 144)

and regarding the children of Israel, He says,

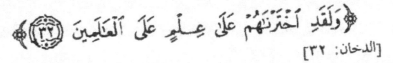

[الدخان: ٣٢]

" And we chose them aforetime above the nations knowingly."

(Al-Dukhan: 32)

It is known that Abraham, peace be upon him, was made better than Moses, and Muhammad, peace and blessings be upon him, was made better than both. By the same token, the Muslim nation has been made better than the ones preceding it in terms of number, knowledge and good deeds.

Again the verse may also mean that Mary was chosen above all women preceding and following her. Some scholars, like Ibn Hazm, state that Mary was a Prophetess, since the angels inspired her. They also state that Sara, the wife of Abraham, peace be upon him, was a Prophetess. However, the majority of scholars maintain that Prophethood is a distinctive feature of men and not women, and that the lofty status of Mary is clarified in Allah's saying,

مَّا الْمَسِيحُ ابْنُ مَرْيَمَ إِلَّا رَسُولٌ قَدْ خَلَتْ
مِن قَبْلِهِ الرُّسُلُ وَأُمُّهُ صِدِّيقَةٌ كَانَا
يَأْكُلَانِ الطَّعَامَ انظُرْ كَيْفَ نُبَيِّنُ لَهُمُ
الْآيَاتِ ثُمَّ انظُرْ أَنَّى يُؤْفَكُونَ ﴿٧٥﴾ [المائدة: ٧٥]

" Christ the son of Mary was no more than a Messenger; many were the Messengers that passed away before him. His mother was a woman of truth."

(Al Maa'idah: 75)

As a matter of fact, Mary is one of the four perfect women, the other three being Asiya, the wife of Pharaoh, Khadeejah, the wife of Prophet Muhammad, and Fatimah, the daughter of Prophet Muhammad.

Ibn `Abbaas reported that the Prophet, peace and blessings be upon him, had drawn four lines and said,

"Do you know what these are?" Thereupon the Companions of the Prophet said, " Allah and His Prophet know best." He answered, " The best women of paradise shall be Khadeejah bint Khuwailid, Fatimah bint Muhammad, Maryam (Mary) bint `Imraan, and Asiya bint Muzahem, the wife of Pharaoh."

Abu Musa Al-Ash`ari also narrated that the Prophet, peace and blessings be upon him, said,

"Perfect men are many, whereas perfect women are only the following: Asiya, the wife of Pharaoh, Mary the daughter of 'Imr'an, and the superiority of `A'ishah to other women is like that of meat to other kinds of food."

The Birth of Jesus (`Eesa), Peace Be upon Him:

وَاذْكُرْ فِي الْكِتَٰبِ مَرْيَمَ إِذِ انتَبَذَتْ مِنْ أَهْلِهَا مَكَانًا شَرْقِيًّا ۝ فَاتَّخَذَتْ مِن دُونِهِمْ حِجَابًا فَأَرْسَلْنَا إِلَيْهَا رُوحَنَا فَتَمَثَّلَ لَهَا بَشَرًا سَوِيًّا ۝ قَالَتْ إِنِّي أَعُوذُ بِالرَّحْمَٰنِ مِنكَ إِن كُنتَ تَقِيًّا ۝ قَالَ إِنَّمَا أَنَا رَسُولُ رَبِّكِ لِأَهَبَ لَكِ غُلَٰمًا زَكِيًّا ۝ قَالَتْ أَنَّىٰ يَكُونُ لِي غُلَٰمٌ وَلَمْ يَمْسَسْنِي بَشَرٌ وَلَمْ أَكُ بَغِيًّا ۝ قَالَ كَذَٰلِكِ قَالَ رَبُّكِ هُوَ عَلَيَّ هَيِّنٌ وَلِنَجْعَلَهُ ءَايَةً لِّلنَّاسِ وَرَحْمَةً مِّنَّا ۚ وَكَانَ أَمْرًا مَّقْضِيًّا ۝ ۞ فَحَمَلَتْهُ فَانتَبَذَتْ بِهِ مَكَانًا قَصِيًّا ۝ فَأَجَآءَهَا الْمَخَاضُ إِلَىٰ جِذْعِ النَّخْلَةِ قَالَتْ يَٰلَيْتَنِي مِتُّ قَبْلَ هَٰذَا وَكُنتُ نَسْيًا مَّنسِيًّا ۝ فَنَادَىٰهَا مِن تَحْتِهَآ أَلَّا تَحْزَنِي قَدْ جَعَلَ رَبُّكِ تَحْتَكِ سَرِيًّا ۝ وَهُزِّي إِلَيْكِ بِجِذْعِ النَّخْلَةِ تُسَٰقِطْ عَلَيْكِ رُطَبًا جَنِيًّا ۝ فَكُلِي وَاشْرَبِي وَقَرِّي عَيْنًا ۖ فَإِمَّا تَرَيِنَّ مِنَ الْبَشَرِ أَحَدًا فَقُولِي إِنِّي نَذَرْتُ لِلرَّحْمَٰنِ صَوْمًا فَلَنْ أُكَلِّمَ الْيَوْمَ إِنسِيًّا ۝ فَأَتَتْ بِهِ قَوْمَهَا تَحْمِلُهُ ۖ قَالُوا يَٰمَرْيَمُ لَقَدْ جِئْتِ شَيْئًا فَرِيًّا ۝ يَٰأُخْتَ هَٰرُونَ مَا كَانَ أَبُوكِ امْرَأَ سَوْءٍ وَمَا كَانَتْ أُمُّكِ بَغِيًّا

فَأَشَارَتْ إِلَيْهِ ﴿٢٨﴾ قَالُوا كَيْفَ نُكَلِّمُ مَن كَانَ فِي
الْمَهْدِ صَبِيًّا ﴿٢٩﴾ قَالَ إِنِّي عَبْدُ اللَّهِ ءَاتَىٰنِيَ الْكِتَٰبَ
وَجَعَلَنِي نَبِيًّا ﴿٣٠﴾ وَجَعَلَنِي مُبَارَكًا أَيْنَ مَا كُنتُ
وَأَوْصَٰنِي بِالصَّلَوٰةِ وَالزَّكَوٰةِ مَا دُمْتُ حَيًّا ﴿٣١﴾ وَبَرًّا
بِوَٰلِدَتِي وَلَمْ يَجْعَلْنِي جَبَّارًا شَقِيًّا ﴿٣٢﴾ وَالسَّلَٰمُ عَلَىَّ
يَوْمَ وُلِدتُّ وَيَوْمَ أَمُوتُ وَيَوْمَ أُبْعَثُ حَيًّا ﴿٣٣﴾
ذَٰلِكَ عِيسَى ابْنُ مَرْيَمَ قَوْلَ الْحَقِّ الَّذِي فِيهِ يَمْتَرُونَ
﴿٣٤﴾ مَا كَانَ لِلَّهِ أَن يَتَّخِذَ مِن وَلَدٍ سُبْحَٰنَهُ إِذَا قَضَىٰ
أَمْرًا فَإِنَّمَا يَقُولُ لَهُ كُن فَيَكُونُ ﴿٣٥﴾ وَإِنَّ اللَّهَ رَبِّي وَرَبُّكُمْ
فَاعْبُدُوهُ هَٰذَا صِرَٰطٌ مُّسْتَقِيمٌ ﴿٣٦﴾ فَاخْتَلَفَ الْأَحْزَابُ
مِنۢ بَيْنِهِمْ فَوَيْلٌ لِّلَّذِينَ كَفَرُوا مِن مَّشْهَدِ يَوْمٍ عَظِيمٍ ﴾

[مريم الآية ١٦ - ٣٧]

"Relate in the Book (the story of) Mary, when she withdrew from her family to a place in the East. She placed a screen (to screen herself) from them; then We sent to her Our angel, and he appeared before her as a man in all respects. She said, ' I seek refuge from thee to (Allah) Most Gracious: (come not near) if thou dost fear Allah.' He said, ' Nay, I am only a Messenger from thy Lord, (to announce) to thee the gift of a holy son.' She said, ' How shall I have a son seeing that no man has touched me and I am not unchaste?' He said, 'So (it will be): thy Lord saith, 'That is easy for Me: and (We *wish) to appoint him as a Sign unto men and a Mercy from Us': it is a matter (so) decreed.' So she conceived him, and she retired with him to a remote place. And the pains of childbirth drove her to the trunk of a palm tree: she cried (in her anguish): 'Ah! Would that I had died before this! Would that I had been a thing forgotten and out of sight!' But (a voice) cried to her frofm beneath the (palm tree), ' Grieve not! For thy Lord hath provided a rivulet beneath thee; and shake towards thyself the trunk of the palm tree; it will let fall fresh ripe dates upon thee. So eat and drink and cool (thine) eye. And if thou dost see any man, say, ' I have vowed a fast to (Allah) Most Gracious, and this day will I enter into no talk with any human being ' At length she brought the (babe) to her people, carrying him (in her arms). They said, ' O Mary! Truly an amazing thing hast thou brought! O sister of Aaron! Thy father was not a man of evil, nor thy mother unchaste!' But she pointed to the babe. They said, ' How can we talk to one who is a child in the cradle? ' He said, 'I am indeed a servant of Allah: He has given me Revelation and made me a Prophet; And He has made me blessed wheresoever I be, and has enjoined on me Prayer and Charity as* long as I live: (He) hath made me kind to my mother, and not overbearing or miserable; so Peace is on me the day I was born, the day that I die, and the Day that I shall be raised up to life (again)'! Such was Jesus the son of Mary: (it is) a statement of truth, about which they (vainly) dispute. It is not befitting to (the majesty of) Allah that He should beget a son. Glory be to Him! When He determines a matter, He only says to it, ' Be, ' and it is. Verily Allah is my Lord and your Lord: Him therefore serve ye: this is a Way that is straight. The sects differ among themselves: and woe to the Unbelievers, because of the (coming) Judgment of a momentous Day!"

(Maryam: 16-37)

Ibn Katheer explains: Allah the Almighty mentions this story after the story of Zechariah which acts as a prelude, leading up to it. Allah similarly mentions the two of them in *Surah* Ali `Imraan within a single context. In *Surah* Al Anbiya', Allah the Almighty says:

﴿وَزَكَرِيَّآ إِذْ نَادَىٰ رَبَّهُ رَبِّ لَا تَذَرْنِي فَرْدًا وَأَنتَ خَيْرُ ٱلْوَٰرِثِينَ ۝ فَٱسْتَجَبْنَا لَهُۥ وَوَهَبْنَا لَهُۥ يَحْيَىٰ وَأَصْلَحْنَا لَهُۥ زَوْجَهُۥٓ إِنَّهُمْ كَانُوا۟ يُسَٰرِعُونَ فِى ٱلْخَيْرَٰتِ وَيَدْعُونَنَا رَغَبًا وَرَهَبًا وَكَانُوا۟ لَنَا خَٰشِعِينَ ۝ وَٱلَّتِىٓ أَحْصَنَتْ

$$\text{فَرْجَهَا فَنَفَخْنَا فِيهَا مِن رُّوحِنَا وَجَعَلْنَاهَا}$$
$$\text{وَابْنَهَا آيَةً لِّلْعَالَمِينَ ۝}$$ [الأنبياء: ٨٩ - ٩١]

"And (remember) Zechariah when he cried to his Lord: ' O my Lord! Leave me not without offspring, though Thou art the best of inheritors.' so We listened to him: and We granted him Yahya: We cured his wife's (barrenness) for him. These (three) were ever quick in emulation in good works; they used to call on Us with love and reverence, and humble themselves before Us. And (remember) her who guarded her chastity: We breathed into her of Our Spirit, and We made her and her son a Sign for all peoples "
(Al Anbiyaa': 89-91)

Thus Allah the Almighty narrates that when the Angels brought the news to Mary, peace be upon her, that Allah had chosen her, and that He will grant her a holy son who will be a gracious, sinless Prophet supported by miracles, she wondered at the possibility of begetting a child without a father, as she did not have a husband. The Angels then told her that Allah is capable of effecting whatsoever He wills. When He decrees a matter, he says to it, *"Be and it is"*. She thus accepted what she was told and yielded to the Will of Allah.

$$\text{وَاذْكُرْ فِي الْكِتَابِ مَرْيَمَ إِذِ انتَبَذَتْ مِنْ أَهْلِهَا مَكَانًا شَرْقِيًّا}$$
$$\text{۝ فَاتَّخَذَتْ مِن دُونِهِمْ حِجَابًا فَأَرْسَلْنَا إِلَيْهَا رُوحَنَا}$$

فَتَمَثَّلَ لَهَا بَشَرًا سَوِيًّا ﴿١٧﴾ قَالَتْ إِنِّي أَعُوذُ بِالرَّحْمَنِ مِنكَ إِن كُنتَ تَقِيًّا ﴿١٨﴾ قَالَ إِنَّمَا أَنَا رَسُولُ رَبِّكِ لِأَهَبَ لَكِ غُلَامًا زَكِيًّا ﴿١٩﴾ قَالَتْ أَنَّى يَكُونُ لِي غُلَامٌ وَلَمْ يَمْسَسْنِي بَشَرٌ وَلَمْ أَكُ بَغِيًّا ﴿٢٠﴾ ﴾ [مريم: ١٦ - ٢٠]

Mary never left the mosque except while menstruating or on account of some necessity such as to get water or food. One day she went out for a particular purpose and *"she withdrew from her family to a place in the East."* She retreated to a place east of the Al-Aqsa Mosque. *"She placed a screen (to screen herself) from them;"* i.e. she went into hiding. Then, Allah sent to her the Holy Spirit, Gabriel, *"and he appeared before her as a man in all respects"* meaning in the form of an utterly perfect man. When she saw him, *"She said, ' I seek refuge from thee to (Allah) Most Gracious: (come not near) if thou dost fear Allah.' "* She suspected that he was after her, so she reminded him of Allah and His inescapable punishment. *"He said, ' Nay, I am only a Messenger from thy Lord,"* that is to say, I am not human being, but an angel sent by Allah to you. *"(To announce) to thee the gift of a holy son.' "* i.e. a holy boy. *"She said, ' How shall I have a son"* meaning how can I give birth to a son *"seeing that no man has touched me"* i.e. when I

have no husband "and I am not unchaste?"
meaning she was never a fornicator.

(Maryam: 16-20)

﴿قَالَ كَذَٰلِكِ قَالَ رَبُّكِ هُوَ عَلَيَّ هَيِّنٌ وَلِنَجْعَلَهُۥ ءَايَةً لِّلنَّاسِ وَرَحْمَةً مِّنَّا وَكَانَ أَمْرًا مَّقْضِيًّا ۞﴾[مريم: ٢١]

The angel answered her, *"He said, 'So (it will be): thy Lord saith, 'That is easy for Me:"* i.e. this would be a simple job for Allah to do. He has power to do whatsoever He wills. *"And (We wish) to appoint him as a Sign unto men"* meaning his creation and birth, peculiar as it is, will be evidence of Allah's ability to effect all kinds of creation, as He, the Almighty, created Adam with no man or woman involved, created Eve from a man with no woman involved, created Jesus from a woman with no man involved and created the rest of the human race from both sexes. *"And a Mercy from Us:"* meaning Jesus will be a means of salvation for people by calling on them to worship only Allah, both as an infant and as an adult. *"It is a matter (so) decreed."*

(Maryam: 21)

This may be the completion of Gabriel's words to Mary, meaning that this issue was decreed and ordained by Allah.

Conversely, it could also be the words of Allah, Exalted be He, addressing his Messenger Muhammad, peace and blessings be upon him, and they refer inadvertently to Gabriel's breathing into her of Allah's Spirit, and Allah the Almighty says in another verse,

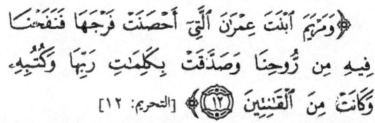

"And Mary the daughter of 'Imran, who guarded her chastity; and We breathed into (her body) of Our spirit; and she testified to the truth of the words of her Lord and of his Revelations, and was one of the Devout (Servants)."

(Al-Taḥrim: 12)

﴿فَحَمَلَتْهُ فَانتَبَذَتْ بِهِۦ مَكَانًا قَصِيًّا ۝﴾ [مريم: ٢٢]

Many of the early Muslims (As-Salaf As-Ṣaaliḥ) mention that Gabriel, peace be upon him, breathed into the pockets of Mary's mail, and that breath found its way to her vulva causing her to conceive right away just as all women do after sexual intercourse with their husbands. *"So she conceived him,"* i.e. she conceived her baby *"and she retired with him to a remote place"* because when Mary, peace be upon her, became pregnant, she was troubled as she knew that many people would doubt her chastity.

(Maryam: 22)

Wahb Ibn Munabih states: When signs of pregnancy began to show on Mary, a man from the Israeli worshippers was first to perceive them. This surprised him immensely, as he was aware she was pious, chaste and devout. One day, he broached the issue to her saying, "Could there be a plant stemming from no seed, Mary?" She answered, "Yes, who created the very first plant?" He answered, "Could a tree grow with no water or rain?" She answered, "Yes, who created the very first tree?" He asked, " Could a child be created without being conceived by a man?" She replied, "Yes, Allah created Adam from no man or woman." He said, "Tell me then your story.

﴿إِذْ قَالَتِ ٱلْمَلَٰٓئِكَةُ يَٰمَرْيَمُ إِنَّ ٱللَّهَ يُبَشِّرُكِ بِكَلِمَةٍ مِّنْهُ ٱسْمُهُ ٱلْمَسِيحُ عِيسَى ٱبْنُ مَرْيَمَ وَجِيهًا فِى ٱلدُّنْيَا وَٱلْءَاخِرَةِ وَمِنَ ٱلْمُقَرَّبِينَ ۝ وَيُكَلِّمُ ٱلنَّاسَ فِى ٱلْمَهْدِ وَكَهْلًا وَمِنَ ٱلصَّٰلِحِينَ ۝﴾ [آل عمران: ٤٥-٤٦]

" She said, "Allah has broken the news to me, "*a word from him: his name will be Christ Jesus. The son of Mary, held in honor in this world and the Hereafter and of (the company of) those nearest to Allah; he shall speak to the people in childhood and in maturity and*

*he shall be (of the company of) of the
righteous."*

(Ali `Imraan: 45-46)

Exegetes of the Qur'an mention: One day Mary
walked by Zechariah's wife who was then expecting a
child; John, after Allah had answered her husband's
prayer. She asked her, "Do you know that I am
pregnant, Mary?" Mary replied, "And do you know that I
am pregnant, too?" Then, she told her about her story and
all that happened to her. Zechariah and his wife were
devout worshippers who had strong faith in Allah. From
that time, whenever Zechariah's wife met Mary, she
would tell her, "I can see my unborn baby (i.e., John,
peace be upon him) kneeling down in prostration to your
unborn baby (i.e. Jesus, peace be upon him)." Ibn
Katheer states: Prostration here signifies submission and
reverence. According to their religion, prostrating
oneself was permitted as a way of greeting. Joseph's
father and brothers prostrated themselves to him.
However, this has been made unlawful in Islam so that
the reverence and glorification of Allah, Exalted be He,
would be unimpaired.

Exegetes of the Qur'an differ as to the duration of
the term of Mary's conception. The majority state that
Mary carried her child to a full term of nine months as all
women do, because had there been a different story, it
would have been mentioned. It was also mentioned that
once she conceived her baby, she gave birth to him. This
is obviously based on the surface meaning of Allah's
verse, *"So she conceived him, and she retired with him
to a remote place. And the pains of childbirth drove her*

to the trunk of a palm tree", "So" here signifies succession.

Muhammad Ibn Is-haaq states: The word spread among the Jews that Mary was pregnant. No people suffered what the people of Zechariah's house did. Some of the unbelievers accused her of having an affair with Joseph Al-Nagaar, a pious man of her relations who used to join her in the mosque worshipping Allah. Thus, Mary went into seclusion, withdrawing from people, and retreated to a faraway place.

Allah the Almighty says,

﴿فَأَجَآءَهَا ٱلۡمَخَاضُ إِلَىٰ جِذۡعِ ٱلنَّخۡلَةِ قَالَتۡ يَٰلَيۡتَنِى مِتُّ قَبۡلَ هَٰذَا وَكُنتُ نَسۡيًا مَّنسِيًّا ٢٣﴾ [سورة مريم، الآية: ٢٣]

"And the pains of childbirth drove her to the trunk of a palm tree:" Ibn Katheer states: Going into labor, Mary sought the trunk of a palm tree for support in the place to which she retreated. Where this place is located was not unanimously agreed upon. It is generally accepted that it is at Bethlehem, eight miles away from Jerusalem. *"She cried (in her anguish):, 'Ah ! Would that I had died before this! Would that I had been a thing forgotten and out of sight.' "* This proves that wishing for death in times of trials is permitted. Mary knew people would doubt her chastity when she would go back home with a baby in her arms, though they knew that she was a pious worshipper who was

constantly in a state of retreat in the mosque, and that she came from a devout family of Prophets. That was why she was extremely troubled that she wished she had died before that time or that she *"had been a thing forgotten and out of sight!"* meaning she wished she was never born at all.

(Maryam: 23)

Allah the Almighty says, *"But (a voice) cried to her from beneath the (palm tree),"* Mujahid and Al-Hasan state that it was her son, Jesus, peace be upon him, who called her, whereas As-Souddyy, Qatadah and Ibn `Abbaas maintain that it was Gabriel, peace be upon him, who did and that the first time Jesus ever talked was in the presence of the people. *"Grieve not! for thy Lord hath provided a rivulet beneath thee;"* Ibn `Abbaas explains that the rivulet is actually a small river. Ibn Katheer maintains: And the majority of scholars agree with him, and that is the most likely interpretation, that *"and shake towards thyself the trunk of the palm tree;"* means resort to it for support *"the trunk of the palm tree;"* It is suggested that it was a dry palm tree; others think that it was a fruitful tree but it is most likely that the tree was not in its fruiting season. Therefore, it was out of Allah's Grace that Mary would find there food and water. *"It will let fall fresh ripe dates upon thee. So eat and drink and cool (thine) eye."* `Amr Ibn Maymoon once explicated this saying that no food is better for a woman undergoing her postnatal bleeding than dry dates and fresh ripe dates, then he recited this verse.

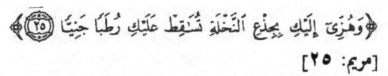

﴿وَهُزِّي إِلَيْكِ بِجِذْعِ ٱلنَّخْلَةِ تُسَٰقِطْ عَلَيْكِ رُطَبًا جَنِيًّا ﴿٢٥﴾﴾

[مريم: ٢٥]

" And if thou dost see any man," Ibn Katheer explains: Allah means if you see anyone, this is the completion of the words of whoever addressed her. *"say,"* to him, i.e. with the aid of signs and gestures, and not using verbal words so as not to be in contradiction to *" 'I have vowed a fast to (Allah) Most Gracious."* By *"a fast"* she meant silence, *"and this day will I enter into no talk with any human being ' "*

(Maryam: 25)

Qatadah and As-Suddyy say, according to their religion, fasting meant abandoning both food and speaking. Ibn Katheer states: Conversely, in Islam, it is not recommended for a fasting person to remain silent all day long.

Allah Almighty says,

﴿فَأَتَتْ بِهِۦ قَوْمَهَا تَحْمِلُهُۥ قَالُوا يَٰمَرْيَمُ لَقَدْ جِئْتِ شَيْئًا فَرِيًّا ﴿٢٧﴾﴾ [مريم: ٢٧]

"At length she brought the (babe) to her people, carrying him (in her arms)." Many of the early Muslims who narrate events and happenings of the People of the Book mention that when her people thought she was missing, they went to ask about her. They stopped by

her dwelling place that was luminous and radiant. When they confronted her, they found her carrying her baby in her arms and told her, *"' O Mary! Truly an amazing thing hast thou brought!' "* Ibn Katheer states that, on the ground of the surface meaning of the context in the Glorious Qur'an, we understand that she carried the child herself and went back to her people with her baby in her arms. Ibn `Abbaas expounds on this saying that that took place forty days after her delivery when her postnatal bleeding came to a stop. When they saw her, they said, *"O Mary! Truly an amazing thing hast thou brought! O sister of Aaron!' "*

(Maryam: 27)

Sa'eed Ibn Gubair says that they likened her to a worshipper of their times called Aaron to whom she was an equal in piety. It is also claimed that the Aaron intended here was Moses' brother and they likened her to him on account of their devoutness. Ibn Katheer says: Muhammad Ibn Ka`b Al-Qarzey was wrong in claiming that she was the sister of Moses and Aaron by kinship, as they lived long before she ever did.

Next they said, *"Thy father was not a man of evil, nor thy mother unchaste!"* meaning you come from a pious family known for their devoutness and righteousness. How could you do something like that? When they accused her of fornication and she was fasting that day, she pointed to her child, meaning they could talk to him. Allah the Almighty says,

﴿يَـٰٓأُخْتَ هَـٰرُونَ مَا كَانَ أَبُوكِ ٱمْرَأَ سَوْءٍ وَمَا كَانَتْ أُمُّكِ بَغِيًّا ۝ فَأَشَارَتْ إِلَيْهِ قَالُوا كَيْفَ نُكَلِّمُ مَن كَانَ فِى ٱلْمَهْدِ صَبِيًّا ۝ قَالَ إِنِّى عَبْدُ ٱللَّهِ ءَاتَـٰنِىَ ٱلْكِتَـٰبَ وَجَعَلَنِى نَبِيًّا ۝﴾ [مريم ٢٨-٣٠]

"But she pointed to the babe. They said, ' *How can we talk to one who is a child in the* *cradle?' "* i.e. how can you refer us to a child who does not understand speech, and he was an infant in his cradle? At this point, *"He* *said, ' I am indeed a servant of Allah:' "* These were the very first words that Jesus, the son of Mary, peace be upon him, ever uttered. He admitted his being a bondman of Allah, and deemed Him far above what stray people might claim, namely that he was the son of Allah. Jesus admitted his being His bondman, Messenger and the son of His maid-servant. Next he acquitted his mother of what those in the dark accused her of and on account of one which they drove her out of town. Thus, he says, *"He has given me Revelation and made* *me a Prophet;"*

(Maryam: 28-30)

$$\{ وَبِكُفْرِهِمْ وَقَوْلِهِمْ عَلَى مَرْيَمَ بُهْتَنًا عَظِيمًا \}$$

$$(١٥٧) \}$$ [النساء: ١٥٦]

"That they rejected Faith; that they uttered against Mary a grave false charge."

(Al Nisaa': 156)

Jesus, peace be upon him, said, *" And He has made me blessed wheresoever I be,"* because he calls on people to worship only Allah Who has no partner, to deem Him far from any defect and from having a wife nor a child. *"And has enjoined on me Prayer and Charity as long as I live:"* It is the duty of the people to perform their obligations towards Allah the Almighty the Praiseworthy by praying and by being charitable to people through paying the Zakah (obligatory charity). This purifies one's soul from vice and purifies one's money and riches by means of giving charity to the needy, who may fall under various categories. Then, he said, *" (He) hath made me kind to my mother"* Many a time has Allah, Exalted be He, linked the commandment to worship Him with that of being dutiful to one's parents. *"And not overbearing or miserable;"* i.e. I am not harsh or coarse. Some of the predecessors say, whoever is not dutiful to his or her parents is always a wretched tyrant.

$$\{ وَالسَّلَمُ عَلَىَّ يَوْمَ وُلِدتُّ وَيَوْمَ أَمُوتُ وَيَوْمَ أُبْعَثُ حَيًّا \}$$

$$(٣٣) \}$$ [مريم: ٣٣]

"So Peace is on me the day I was born, the day that I die, and the Day that I shall be raised up to life (again)'!"

(Maryam: 33)

This is an evidence of his servitude to Allah, Exalted be He, and a proof that he, like all other creatures, lives, dies and will be resurrected. However, Allah ensured his safety through the very three stages, which are quite difficult for all people.

Then, Allah tells His Messenger Muhammad, peace and blessings be upon him, all having narrated to him the story of Jesus, peace be upon him,

$$﴿ذَٰلِكَ عِيسَى ٱبْنُ مَرْيَمَ قَوْلَ ٱلْحَقِّ ٱلَّذِى فِيهِ يَمْتَرُونَ ۝ مَا كَانَ لِلَّهِ أَن يَتَّخِذَ مِن وَلَدٍ سُبْحَٰنَهُۥٓ إِذَا قَضَىٰٓ أَمْرًا فَإِنَّمَا يَقُولُ لَهُۥ كُن فَيَكُونُ ۝﴾ [مريم: ٣٤ - ٣٥]$$

" Such was Jesus the son of Mary: (it is) a statement of truth, about which they (vainly) dispute." i.e. he is Allah's bondman born to a woman who, too, is Allah's bondman. Then, He deemed His Sacred Self far and above all defect. He says, *"It is not befitting to (the majesty of) Allah that He should beget a son. Glory be to Him! When He determines a matter, He only says to it, ' Be, ' and it is."*

(Maryam: 34-35)

meaning nothing is beyond His ability, He is the Sure Accomplisher of what He wills. Similarly, Allah says in another verse,

$$\{ \text{إِنَّ مَثَلَ عِيسَىٰ عِندَ اللَّهِ كَمَثَلِ ءَادَمَ خَلَقَهُ} $$

$$\text{مِن تُرَابٍ ثُمَّ قَالَ لَهُ كُن فَيَكُونُ} \circledast \text{الْحَقُّ مِن رَّبِّكَ}$$

$$\text{فَلَا تَكُن مِّنَ الْمُمْتَرِينَ} \circledast \} \quad [\text{آل عمران: ٥٩ ـ ٦٠}]$$

*"The Truth (comes) from thy Lord alone; so
be not of those who doubt."*

(Ali `Imraan: 59-60)

Jesus, peace be upon him, said,

$$\{ \text{وَإِنَّ اللَّهَ رَبِّي وَرَبُّكُمْ فَاعْبُدُوهُ هَٰذَا صِرَاطٌ مُّسْتَقِيمٌ} \circledast \}$$

$$[\text{مريم: ٣٦}]$$

*"Verily Allah is my Lord and your Lord: Him
therefore serve ye: this is a Way that is
straight."* This is the completion of his words
to the people while in the cradle. He told
them that Allah is his and their god and
ordered them to worship Him. Allah the
Almighty says, *"The sects differ among
themselves:"*

(Maryam: 36)

People of the Book were of various views regarding
Jesus. A group of them, namely the majority of the Jews,
insisted that he was a bastard child. They persisted in
their atheism and obstinacy and were severely cursed by
Allah. Another group maintained that Jesus is God. He
came down to earth, brought back to life some people,
took the lives of others and then went back to heaven.
This is the view of the Jacobites. Others, namely the

Nestorians, claim that Jesus is the son of Allah. Others still maintained that Jesus is the third party of the Trinity: Allah is a god, he is a god, and his mother is a god. They are the Israelites, kings of the Christians. Others believe, he is Allah's bondman, Messenger, spirit and word. This view is adopted by the Muslims.

Allah Almighty says,

$$﴿فَاخْتَلَفَ الْأَحْزَابُ مِنْ بَيْنِهِمْ فَوَيْلٌ لِّلَّذِينَ كَفَرُوا مِنْ مَشْهَدِ يَوْمٍ عَظِيمٍ (٣٧)﴾ [مريم الآية: ٣٧]$$

"and woe to the Unbelievers, because of the (coming) Judgment of a momentous Day!"

(Maryam: 37)

This is a strong threat and an ultimatum to whoever ascribes false allegations to Allah claiming He has a son. Allah the Almighty has given them a deadline till the Day of Judgment out of patience and confidence in His ability to subdue them. Allah, Exalted be He, never hastens the punishment of those who disobey him. Thus, it was mentioned in the two authentic books that Allah's Messenger, peace and blessings be upon him, said,

"Allah gives respite to a "zalim" (polytheist, wrong-doer, oppressors, etc.) but when He seizes (catches) him, He never releases him."

Then Abu Musa, the narrator, may Allah be pleased with him, recited,

$$﴿وَكَذَلِكَ أَخْذُ رَبِّكَ إِذَا أَخَذَ الْقُرَى وَهِيَ ظَالِمَةٌ إِنَّ أَخْذَهُ أَلِيمٌ شَدِيدٌ (١٠٢)﴾ [هود: ١٠٢]$$

"Such is the Seizure of your Lord when He seizes the (population of) towns while they are doing wrong: Verily, His seizure is painful, and severe. "

(Hood: 102)

It is also mentioned in the two <u>Sahihs</u> that Allah's Messenger, peace and blessings be upon him said,

"No one is more forbearing in listening to the most irksome things than Allah, the Exalted. They associate rivals with Him, attribute sonhood to Him but in spite of this He provides them with sustenance, grants them safety, confers upon them so many things."

﴿وَلَا تَحْسَبَنَّ ٱللَّهَ غَافِلًا عَمَّا يَعْمَلُ ٱلظَّٰلِمُونَ إِنَّمَا يُؤَخِّرُهُمْ لِيَوْمٍ تَشْخَصُ فِيهِ ٱلْأَبْصَٰرُ ﴿٤٣﴾ [إبراهيم: ٤٢]

"Think not that Allah doth not heed the deeds of those who do wrong. He but giveth them respite against a Day when the eyes will fixedly stare in horror."

(Ibraheem: 42)

Al-Bu<u>kh</u>ari reports on the authority of `Ubadah Ibn As-<u>S</u>aamit that the Prophet, peace and blessings be upon him, said,

" If anyone testifies that none has the right to be worshipped but Allah alone, Who has no partners, and that Mu<u>h</u>ammad, peace and

blessings be upon him, is His slave and His Messenger, and that 'Eesa (Jesus), peace be upon him, is Allah's slave and His Messenger and His Word ("Be," and he was) which He bestowed on Maryam (Mary) and a Rooh (spirit) created by Him, and that Paradise, is the truth and Hell is the truth, Allah will admit him into Paradise with the deeds which he had done even if those deeds were few. "

After Allah, Exalted be He, has mentioned the story of Jesus, peace be upon him, in *Surah* Ali 'Imraan, He says,

﴿ذَلِكَ نَتْلُوهُ عَلَيْكَ مِنَ ٱلْآيَٰتِ وَٱلذِّكْرِ ٱلْحَكِيمِ ۝٥٨ إِنَّ مَثَلَ عِيسَىٰ عِندَ ٱللَّهِ كَمَثَلِ ءَادَمَّ خَلَقَهُ مِن تُرَابٍ ثُمَّ قَالَ لَهُۥ كُن فَيَكُونُ ۝٥٩ ٱلْحَقُّ مِن رَّبِّكَ فَلَا تَكُن مِّنَ ٱلْمُمْتَرِينَ ۝٦٠ فَمَنْ حَاجَّكَ فِيهِ مِنْ بَعْدِ مَا جَآءَكَ مِنَ ٱلْعِلْمِ فَقُلْ تَعَالَوْا۟ نَدْعُ أَبْنَآءَنَا وَأَبْنَآءَكُمْ وَنِسَآءَنَا وَنِسَآءَكُمْ وَأَنفُسَنَا وَأَنفُسَكُمْ ثُمَّ نَبْتَهِلْ فَنَجْعَل لَّعْنَتَ ٱللَّهِ عَلَى ٱلْكَٰذِبِينَ ۝٦١ إِنَّ هَٰذَا لَهُوَ ٱلْقَصَصُ ٱلْحَقُّ وَمَا مِنْ إِلَٰهٍ إِلَّا ٱللَّهُ وَإِنَّ ٱللَّهَ لَهُوَ ٱلْعَزِيزُ ٱلْحَكِيمُ ۝٦٢ فَإِن تَوَلَّوْا۟ فَإِنَّ ٱللَّهَ عَلِيمٌۢ بِٱلْمُفْسِدِينَ ۝٦٣﴾ [آل عمران: ٥٨ ـ ٦٣]

"This is what we rehearse unto thee of the Signs and the Message of Wisdom. The similitude of Jesus before Allah is as that of Adam; he created him from dust, then said to him: "Be": and he was. The Truth (comes) from thy Lord alone; so be not of those who

doubt. If anyone disputes in this matter with thee, now after (full) knowledge hath come to thee, say: "Come! Let us gather together - our sons and your sons, our women and your women, ourselves and yourselves: then let us earnestly pray, and invoke the curse of Allah on those who lie! This is the true account; there is no god except Allah; and Allah - He is indeed the Exalted in power, the Wise. But if they turn back, Allah has full knowledge of those who do mischief."

(Ali `Imraan: 58-63)

That is why the Najraan delegation came to meet our Prophet, Muhammad, peace and blessings be upon him, and they were sixty in number, with fourteen of them in charge of all the rest, while the entire group had three chiefs, who were the noblest and the most highborn among them. They were, Al- `Aaqib, As-Sayyid and Abu Haarithah Ibn 'Alqamah. The three of them kept deliberating on Jesus. Therefore, Allah revealed *Surah Ali Imraan* which tackled this issue. Allah explained how Jesus was created and how his mother had been created earlier. Allah also commanded his Prophet Muhammad, peace and blessings be upon him, to invoke the curse of Allah on them if they did not obey him and embrace Islam.

They reverted to reconciliation and truce. One of the delegation, Al-`Aaqib `Abdel Maseeh, addressed the rest saying, "Christian brothers, you have come to know that Muhammad is a Prophet sent by Allah and that he has told you the truth about your Prophet, Jesus. You are also aware of the fact that whenever people curse a Prophet, their elite start to decline and their promising blossoms are eradicated. To curse the Prophet then is to bring demolition upon yourselves. So if you insist on maintaining your religion and persisting in your claims about your Prophet, make peace with the man and go back home. So they asked so of Allah's Messenger, peace and blessings be upon him, asked him to name the *Jizya*[1] he was to levy on them, and to send with them a trustworthy man. So he sent Abu Ubaidah Al-Garraah, a story which was narrated in detail in the biography of the Prophet.

---

[1] *JJizya* is a poll tax levied from those who do not accept Islam but are willing to live under the protection of the Islamic state.

Allah, Exalted Be He, Is Far and Above Having a Child

Allah the Almighty says,

﴿وَقَالُوا اتَّخَذَ الرَّحْمَٰنُ وَلَدًا ۝ لَّقَدْ جِئْتُمْ شَيْئًا إِدًّا ۝ تَكَادُ السَّمَاوَاتُ يَتَفَطَّرْنَ مِنْهُ وَتَنشَقُّ الْأَرْضُ وَتَخِرُّ الْجِبَالُ هَدًّا ۝ أَن دَعَوْا لِلرَّحْمَٰنِ وَلَدًا ۝ وَمَا يَنبَغِي لِلرَّحْمَٰنِ أَن يَتَّخِذَ وَلَدًا ۝ إِن كُلُّ مَن فِي السَّمَاوَاتِ وَالْأَرْضِ إِلَّا آتِي الرَّحْمَٰنِ عَبْدًا ۝ لَّقَدْ أَحْصَاهُمْ وَعَدَّهُمْ عَدًّا ۝ وَكُلُّهُمْ آتِيهِ يَوْمَ الْقِيَامَةِ فَرْدًا ۝﴾ [مريم الآية ٨٨ ـ ٩٥]

" They say: (Allah) Most Gracious has begotten a son! Indeed ye have put forth a thing most monstrous!" i.e. a colossal sin, *"As if the skies are ready to burst, the earth to split asunder, and the mountains to fall down in utter ruin. That they should invoke a son for (Allah) Most Gracious. For it is not consonant with the majesty of (Allah) Most Gracious that He should beget a son. Not one of the beings in the heavens and the earth but must come to (Allah) Most Gracious as a servant. He does take an account of them (all), and hath numbered*

them (all) exactly. And every one of them will come to Him singly on the Day of Judgement."

(Maryam: 88-95)

Allah, Exalted be He, explains that He can have no child as He is the Creator and Owner of everything and all are in need of Him. All creatures in heaven and on earth are His bondmen. He is their sole god.

Allah the Almighty says,

﴿وَجَعَلُوا لِلَّهِ شُرَكَاءَ الْجِنَّ وَخَلَقَهُمْ وَخَرَقُوا لَهُ بَنِينَ وَبَنَاتٍ بِغَيْرِ عِلْمٍ سُبْحَانَهُ وَتَعَالَى عَمَّا يَصِفُونَ ۝ بَدِيعُ السَّمَوَاتِ وَالْأَرْضِ أَنَّى يَكُونُ لَهُ وَلَدٌ وَلَمْ تَكُن لَّهُ صَاحِبَةٌ وَخَلَقَ كُلَّ شَيْءٍ وَهُوَ بِكُلِّ شَيْءٍ عَلِيمٌ ۝ ذَلِكُمُ اللَّهُ رَبُّكُمْ لَا إِلَهَ إِلَّا هُوَ خَالِقُ كُلِّ شَيْءٍ فَاعْبُدُوهُ وَهُوَ عَلَى كُلِّ شَيْءٍ وَكِيلٌ ۝ لَا تُدْرِكُهُ الْأَبْصَارُ وَهُوَ يُدْرِكُ الْأَبْصَارَ وَهُوَ اللَّطِيفُ الْخَبِيرُ ۝﴾ [الأنعام: ١٠٠ - ١٠٣]

" Yet they make the Jinns equals with Allah, though Allah did create the Jinns; and they falsely, having no knowledge, attribute to him sons and daughters. Praise and glory be to Him! (for He is) above what they attribute to Him! To Him is due the primal origin of the heavens and the earth: how can He have

a son when He has no consort? He created all things, and He has full knowledge of all things. That is Allah, your Lord! There is no god but He, the Creator of all things; then worship ye Him; and He hath power to dispose of all affairs. No vision can grasp Him. But His grasp is over all vision: He is above all comprehension, yet is acquainted in all things."

(Al An`aam: 100-103)

Allah thus explains that He is the Creator of everything, He is Unique, and therefore can never have a child.

Allah the Almighty says, *"Say:*

He is Allah, the One and Only;" i.e. Allah is peerless, *"Allah, the Eternal, Absolute;"* i.e. He is the Master Whose Knowledge, Wisdom and Mercy are perfect, *"He begetteth not,"* i.e. He has no child, *"Nor is He begotten;"* i.e. He was not born, *"And there is none like unto Him."* meaning He has no equal, thus Allah can never have a child.

(Al Ikhlaas)

﴿يَـٰٓأَهْلَ ٱلْكِتَـٰبِ لَا تَغْلُوا۟ فِى دِينِكُمْ وَلَا تَقُولُوا۟ عَلَى ٱللَّهِ إِلَّا ٱلْحَقَّ إِنَّمَا ٱلْمَسِيحُ عِيسَى ٱبْنُ مَرْيَمَ رَسُولُ ٱللَّهِ وَكَلِمَتُهُۥ أَلْقَىٰهَآ إِلَىٰ مَرْيَمَ وَرُوحٌ مِّنْهُ فَـَٔامِنُوا۟ بِٱللَّهِ وَرُسُلِهِۦ وَلَا تَقُولُوا۟ ثَلَـٰثَةٌ ٱنتَهُوا۟ خَيْرًا لَّكُمْ إِنَّمَا ٱللَّهُ إِلَـٰهٌ وَٰحِدٌ سُبْحَـٰنَهُۥٓ أَن يَكُونَ لَهُۥ وَلَدٌ لَّهُۥ مَا فِى ٱلسَّمَـٰوَٰتِ وَمَا فِى ٱلْأَرْضِ وَكَفَىٰ بِٱللَّهِ وَكِيلًا ۝ لَّن يَسْتَنكِفَ ٱلْمَسِيحُ أَن يَكُونَ عَبْدًا لِّلَّهِ وَلَا ٱلْمَلَـٰٓئِكَةُ ٱلْمُقَرَّبُونَ وَمَن يَسْتَنكِفْ عَنْ عِبَادَتِهِۦ وَيَسْتَكْبِرْ فَسَيَحْشُرُهُمْ إِلَيْهِ جَمِيعًا ۝ فَأَمَّا ٱلَّذِينَ ءَامَنُوا۟ وَعَمِلُوا۟ ٱلصَّـٰلِحَـٰتِ فَيُوَفِّيهِمْ أُجُورَهُمْ وَيَزِيدُهُم مِّن فَضْلِهِۦ وَأَمَّا ٱلَّذِينَ ٱسْتَنكَفُوا۟ وَٱسْتَكْبَرُوا۟ فَيُعَذِّبُهُمْ عَذَابًا أَلِيمًا وَلَا يَجِدُونَ لَهُم مِّن دُونِ ٱللَّهِ وَلِيًّا وَلَا نَصِيرًا ۝﴾ [النساء: ١٧١ - ١٧٣]

"O People of the Book! Commit no excesses in your religion: nor say of Allah aught but the truth. Christ Jesus the son, Mary was (no more than) a Messenger of Allah and His Word, which He bestowed on Mary, and a Spirit proceeding from Him: so believe in Allah and His Messengers. Say not ' Trinity': desist: it will be better for you: for Allah is One God: glory be to Him: (far

Exalted is He) above having a son. To Him belongeth all things in the heavens and on earth. And enough is Allah as a Disposer of affairs. Christ disdains not to serve and worship Allah, nor do the angels, those nearest (to Allah): those who disdain his worship and are arrogant - he will gather them all together unto Himself to (answer). But to those who believe and do deeds of righteousness, He will give their (due) rewards - and more, out of His bounty: but those who are disdainful and arrogant, He will punish with a grievous penalty; nor will they find, besides Allah, any to protect or help them. "

(Al Nisaa': 171-173)

Allah forbids the People of the Book to go to extremes in religion. Christians' praise of Jesus is exaggerated. They should have adhered only to the fact that he is Allah's bondman and Messenger and the son of the Virgin who kept her chastity and to whom Allah sent Gabriel who breathed into her of Allah's spirit, upon Allah's command, causing her to conceive. Mary was actually in contact with the Divine Spirit through Gabriel. However, she is one of Allah's creatures and Jesus' name was habitually attached to hers as he had no father. Allah the Almighty says,

﴿إِنَّ مَثَلَ عِيسَىٰ عِندَ اللَّهِ كَمَثَلِ ءَادَمَ خَلَقَهُ مِن تُرَابٍ ثُمَّ قَالَ لَهُۥ كُن فَيَكُونُ ٥٩﴾ [آل عمران: ٥٩]

" The similitude of Jesus before Allah is as that of Adam; He created him from dust, then said to him: ' Be ': and he was."

(Ali `Imraan: 59)

Likewise, Allah says,

﴿وَقَالُوا اتَّخَذَ اللَّهُ وَلَدًا سُبْحَانَهُ بَل لَّهُ مَا فِي السَّمَاوَاتِ وَالْأَرْضِ كُلٌّ لَّهُ قَانِتُونَ ۝ بَدِيعُ السَّمَاوَاتِ وَالْأَرْضِ وَإِذَا قَضَى أَمْرًا فَإِنَّمَا يَقُولُ لَهُ كُن فَيَكُونُ ۝﴾ [البقرة: ١١٦ - ١١٧]

"They say, 'Allah hath begotten a son': Glory be to Him - Nay, to Him belongs all that is in the heavens and on earth: everything renders worship to Him. To Him is due the primal origin of the heavens and the earth when He decreeth a matter, He says to it: ' Be, ' and it is."

(Al Baqarah: 116-117)

Allah the Almighty says,

﴿وَقَالَتِ الْيَهُودُ عُزَيْرٌ ابْنُ اللَّهِ وَقَالَتِ النَّصَارَى الْمَسِيحُ ابْنُ اللَّهِ ذَلِكَ قَوْلُهُم بِأَفْوَاهِهِمْ يُضَاهِئُونَ قَوْلَ الَّذِينَ كَفَرُوا مِن قَبْلُ قَاتَلَهُمُ اللَّهُ أَنَّى يُؤْفَكُونَ ۝﴾ [التوبة: ٣٠]

"The Jews call `Uzair (Ezra) a son of God, and the Christians call Christ the Son of God. That is a saying from their mouth; (in this) they but imitate what the Unbelievers of old used to say. Allah's curse be on them: how they are deluded away from the Truth!"

(Al Tawbah: 30)

Allah states that the Jews and the Christians having both falsely claimed that Allah has a child, far and above be He from all that. Allah explains that their allegations are baseless.

Similarly, many sects of the Arabs claimed out of ignorance that the angels are the daughters of Allah and that He married into the Jinns and begot angels for daughters. Far be He from these false claims. Allah the Almighty says,

﴿وَجَعَلُوا الْمَلَٰئِكَةَ الَّذِينَ هُمْ عِبَٰدُ الرَّحْمَٰنِ إِنَٰثًا أَشَهِدُوا خَلْقَهُمْ سَتُكْتَبُ شَهَٰدَتُهُمْ وَيُسْـَٔلُونَ ﴿١٩﴾﴾ [الزخرف: ١٩]

"And they make into females angels who themselves serve Allah. Did they witness their creation? Their evidence will be recorded, and they will be called to account!"

(Al Zukhruf: 19)

Allah the Almighty says,

﴿ فَٱسْتَفْتِهِمْ أَلِرَبِّكَ ٱلْبَنَاتُ وَلَهُمُ ٱلْبَنُونَ ۝ (١٤٩) أَمْ خَلَقْنَا ٱلْمَلَٰٓئِكَةَ إِنَٰثًا وَهُمْ شَٰهِدُونَ ۝ (١٥٠) أَلَآ إِنَّهُم مِّنْ إِفْكِهِمْ لَيَقُولُونَ ۝ (١٥١) وَلَدَ ٱللَّهُ وَإِنَّهُمْ لَكَٰذِبُونَ ۝ (١٥٢) أَصْطَفَى ٱلْبَنَاتِ عَلَى ٱلْبَنِينَ ۝ (١٥٣) مَا لَكُمْ كَيْفَ تَحْكُمُونَ ۝ (١٥٤) أَفَلَا تَذَكَّرُونَ ۝ (١٥٥) أَمْ لَكُمْ سُلْطَٰنٌ مُّبِينٌ ۝ (١٥٦) فَأْتُوا بِكِتَٰبِكُمْ إِن كُنتُمْ صَٰدِقِينَ ۝ (١٥٧) وَجَعَلُوا بَيْنَهُ وَبَيْنَ ٱلْجِنَّةِ نَسَبًا وَلَقَدْ عَلِمَتِ ٱلْجِنَّةُ إِنَّهُمْ لَمُحْضَرُونَ ۝ (١٥٨) سُبْحَٰنَ ٱللَّهِ عَمَّا يَصِفُونَ ۝ (١٥٩) إِلَّا عِبَادَ ٱللَّهِ ٱلْمُخْلَصِينَ ۝ (١٦٠) ﴾ [الصافات الآية ١٤٩ ـ ١٦٠]

"Now ask them their opinion: is it that thy Lord has (only) daughters, and they have sons? - Or that We created the angels female, and they are witnesses upon (thereto)? Is it not that may say, from their own invention, ' Allah has begotten children '? But they are liars! Did He (then) choose daughters rather than sons? What is the matter with you? How judge ye? Will ye not then receive admonition? Or have ye an authority manifest? Then bring ye your Book (of authority) if ye be Truthful! And they have invented a blood relationship between Him and the Jinns: but the Jinns know (quite well) that they have indeed to appear (before His Judgment Seat)! Glory to Allah! (He is

*free) from the things they ascribe (to Him)!
Not (so do) the Servants of Allah, sincere
and devoted. "*

(Al Saaffaat: 149-160)

Allah, Exalted be He, says in another *Surah*,

﴿وَقَالُوا اتَّخَذَ الرَّحْمَنُ وَلَدًا سُبْحَانَهُ بَلْ عِبَادٌ
مُّكْرَمُونَ ۝ لَا يَسْبِقُونَهُ بِالْقَوْلِ وَهُم بِأَمْرِهِ
يَعْمَلُونَ ۝ يَعْلَمُ مَا بَيْنَ أَيْدِيهِمْ وَمَا خَلْفَهُمْ وَلَا
يَشْفَعُونَ إِلَّا لِمَنِ ارْتَضَى وَهُم مِّنْ خَشْيَتِهِ مُشْفِقُونَ
۝ وَمَن يَقُلْ مِنْهُمْ إِنِّي إِلَهٌ مِّن دُونِهِ فَذَلِكَ
نَجْزِيهِ جَهَنَّمَ كَذَلِكَ نَجْزِي الظَّالِمِينَ ۝﴾

[الأنبياء: ٢٦ - ٢٩]

*"And they say: ' (Allah) Most Gracious has
begotten offspring. ' Glory to Him! They are
(but) servants raised to honor. They speak
not before He speaks, and they act (in all
things) by His command. He knows what is
before them, and what is behind them, and
they offer no intercession except for those
who are acceptable, and they stand in awe
and reverence of His (glory). If any of them
should say, ' I am a god besides Him' such a
one We should reward with Hell: thus do We
reward those who do wrong. "*

(Al Anbiyaa': 26-29)

Allah, Exalted be He, says in the opening of *Surah Al Kahf*,

﴿ٱلْحَمْدُ لِلَّهِ ٱلَّذِىٓ أَنزَلَ عَلَىٰ عَبْدِهِ ٱلْكِتَٰبَ وَلَمْ يَجْعَل لَّهُۥ عِوَجَا ۜ ۝ قَيِّمًا لِّيُنذِرَ بَأْسًا شَدِيدًا مِّن لَّدُنْهُ وَيُبَشِّرَ ٱلْمُؤْمِنِينَ ٱلَّذِينَ يَعْمَلُونَ ٱلصَّٰلِحَٰتِ أَنَّ لَهُمْ أَجْرًا حَسَنًا ۝ مَّٰكِثِينَ فِيهِ أَبَدًا ۝ وَيُنذِرَ ٱلَّذِينَ قَالُوا۟ ٱتَّخَذَ ٱللَّهُ وَلَدًا ۝ مَّا لَهُم بِهِۦ مِنْ عِلْمٍ وَلَا لِءَابَآئِهِمْ ۚ كَبُرَتْ كَلِمَةً تَخْرُجُ مِنْ أَفْوَٰهِهِمْ ۚ إِن يَقُولُونَ إِلَّا كَذِبًا ۝﴾ [الكهف الآية ١ - ٥]

"Praise be to Allah, Who hath sent to His Bondman the Book, and has allowed therein no crookedness: (He hath made it) Straight (and Clear) in order that He may warn (the godless) of a terrible Punishment from Him, and that He may give Glad Tidings to the Believers who work righteous deeds, that they shall have a goodly Reward. Wherein they shall remain forever: further, that He may warn those (also) who say, ' Allah has begotten a son': no knowledge have they of such a thing, nor had their fathers. It is a grievous thing that issues from their mouths as a saying. What they say is nothing but falsehoods!"

(Al Kahf: 1-5)

Allah Almighty also says,

﴿هُوَ ٱلَّذِى جَعَلَ لَكُمُ ٱلَّيْلَ لِتَسْكُنُوا۟ فِيهِ وَٱلنَّهَارَ مُبْصِرًا إِنَّ فِى ذَٰلِكَ لَءَايَٰتٍ لِّقَوْمٍ يَسْمَعُونَ ۝ قَالُوا۟ ٱتَّخَذَ ٱللَّهُ وَلَدًا سُبْحَٰنَهُ هُوَ ٱلْغَنِىُّ لَهُ مَا فِى ٱلسَّمَٰوَٰتِ وَمَا فِى ٱلْأَرْضِ إِنْ عِندَكُم مِّن سُلْطَٰنٍ بِهَٰذَآ أَتَقُولُونَ عَلَى ٱللَّهِ مَا لَا تَعْلَمُونَ ۝ قُلْ إِنَّ ٱلَّذِينَ يَفْتَرُونَ عَلَى ٱللَّهِ ٱلْكَذِبَ لَا يُفْلِحُونَ ۝ مَتَٰعٌ فِى ٱلدُّنْيَا ثُمَّ إِلَيْنَا مَرْجِعُهُمْ ثُمَّ نُذِيقُهُمُ ٱلْعَذَابَ ٱلشَّدِيدَ بِمَا كَانُوا۟ يَكْفُرُونَ ۝﴾ [يونس الآية ٦٧ ــ ٧٠]

"He it is that hath made you the Night that ye may rest therein, and the Day to make things visible (to you). Verily in this are Signs for those who listen (to His Message). They say, ' Allah has begotten a son!' - Glory be to Him! He is Self-Sufficient! His are all things in the heavens and on earth! No warrant have ye for this! Say ye about Allah what ye know not? Say: ' Those who invent a lie against Allah will never prosper.' A little enjoyment in this world! - and then, to Us will be their return. Then shall We

make than taste the severest Penalty for their
blasphemies. "

(Yoonus: 67-70)

These verses refute all false claims of the various atheist sects, namely the philosophers, Arab disbelievers, Jews, Christians who put forth baseless allegations, far be Allah from all that those people ascribe to Him.

Since this particular allegation was mainly made by the Christians, they are frequently referred to in the Qur'an in order to refute their allegation, and to highlight their contradiction and ignorance. As for the truth, it never varies. Allah the Almighty says, *"Do they not consider the Qur'an (with care)? Had it been from other than Allah, they would surely have found therein much discrepancy."* A group of stray people, who were in the dark from amongst them claimed that Jesus is God, another group maintained that he is the son of God, whereas a third group yet thought he is the third party of the Trinity.

In *Surah* Al Maa'idah, Allah the Almighty says,

﴿لَقَدْ كَفَرَ ٱلَّذِينَ قَالُوٓاْ إِنَّ ٱللَّهَ هُوَ ٱلْمَسِيحُ ٱبْنُ مَرْيَمَ قُلْ فَمَن يَمْلِكُ مِنَ ٱللَّهِ شَيْئًا إِنْ أَرَادَ أَن يُهْلِكَ ٱلْمَسِيحَ ٱبْنَ مَرْيَمَ وَأُمَّهُ وَمَن فِي ٱلْأَرْضِ جَمِيعًا وَلِلَّهِ مُلْكُ ٱلسَّمَٰوَٰتِ وَٱلْأَرْضِ وَمَا بَيْنَهُمَا يَخْلُقُ مَا يَشَآءُ وَٱللَّهُ عَلَىٰ كُلِّ شَيْءٍ قَدِيرٌ ﴿١٧﴾﴾ [المائدة: ١٧]

" In blasphemy indeed are those that say that Allah is Christ the son of Mary. Say: ' Who then hath the least power against Allah, if His Will were to destroy Christ the son of Mary, his mother, and all - everyone that is on the earth? For to Allah belongeth the dominion of the heavens and the earth, and all that is between. He createth what He pleaseth. For, Allah hath power over all things. "

(Al Maa'idah: 17)

Allah speaks of their atheism and ignorance. He explains that he is the Creator, and the Powerful.

Towards the end of this *Surah*, Allah the Almighty says,

﴿لَقَدْ كَفَرَ ٱلَّذِينَ قَالُوٓاْ إِنَّ ٱللَّهَ هُوَ ٱلْمَسِيحُ ٱبْنُ مَرْيَمَ وَقَالَ ٱلْمَسِيحُ يَٰبَنِيٓ إِسْرَٰٓءِيلَ ٱعْبُدُواْ ٱللَّهَ رَبِّي وَرَبَّكُمْ إِنَّهُۥ مَن يُشْرِكْ بِٱللَّهِ فَقَدْ حَرَّمَ ٱللَّهُ عَلَيْهِ ٱلْجَنَّةَ وَمَأْوَىٰهُ ٱلنَّارُ وَمَا لِلظَّٰلِمِينَ مِنْ أَنصَارٍ ﴾ ﴿٧٢﴾ [المائدة: ٧٢]

"They do blaspheme who say: ' Allah is Christ the son of Mary.' But said Christ: 'O Children of Israel! Worship Allah, my Lord and your Lord.' " Allah has declared them atheists. He explains how they behaved so though He had sent them Jesus son of Mary,

and though Jesus explained that he was a bondman of Allah and that he was to call on people to worship only Him and to warn those who disobey him that they would be punished in Hell. That is why Allah says, *"Whoever joins other gods with Allah - Allah will forbid him the Garden, and the Fire will be his abode. There will for the wrongdoers be no one to help."*

(Al Maa'idah: 72)

Next, Allah the Almighty says,

$$\text{﴿لَّقَدْ كَفَرَ ٱلَّذِينَ قَالُوٓاْ إِنَّ ٱللَّهَ ثَالِثُ ثَلَٰثَةٍ وَمَا مِنْ إِلَٰهٍ إِلَّآ إِلَٰهٌ وَٰحِدٌ وَإِن لَّمْ يَنتَهُواْ عَمَّا يَقُولُونَ لَيَمَسَّنَّ ٱلَّذِينَ كَفَرُواْ مِنْهُمْ عَذَابٌ أَلِيمٌ ۝ أَفَلَا يَتُوبُونَ إِلَى ٱللَّهِ وَيَسْتَغْفِرُونَهُۥ وَٱللَّهُ غَفُورٌ رَّحِيمٌ ۝﴾}$$

[المائدة: ٧٣ـ ٧٤]

"They do blaspheme who say: Allah is one of three in a Trinity: for there is no god except One God." i.e. He has no partner, no match, no wife or child. Then He warns them saying, *"If they desist not from their word (of blasphemy), verily a grievous penalty will befall the blasphemers among them."* Next, He calls on them gently and mercifully to repent of such a colossal sin that would incur punishment in Hell. He says, *"Why turn they not to Allah and seek His forgiveness? For*

55

Allah is Oft-Forgiving, Most Merciful. "

(Al Maa'idah: 73-74)

Next, Allah speaks in detail about Jesus and his mother explaining that he is a Messenger and that his mother is worthy of praise. He says,

﴿مَّا ٱلْمَسِيحُ ٱبْنُ مَرْيَمَ إِلَّا رَسُولٌ قَدْ خَلَتْ مِن قَبْلِهِ ٱلرُّسُلُ وَأُمُّهُ صِدِّيقَةٌ كَانَا يَأْكُلَانِ ٱلطَّعَامَ ٱنظُرْ كَيْفَ نُبَيِّنُ لَهُمُ ٱلْآيَتِ ثُمَّ ٱنظُرْ أَنَّىٰ يُؤْفَكُونَ ﴿٧٥﴾﴾ [المائدة: ٧٥]

"Christ, the son of Mary, was no more than a Messenger; many were the Messengers that passed away before him. His mother was a woman of truth. They had both to eat their (daily) food. See how Allah doth make His signs clear to them; yet see in what way they are deluded away from the truth!"

(Al Maa'idah: 75)

How can Jesus then be a god?

At the end of this *Surah*, Allah the Almighty says,

﴿وَإِذْ قَالَ ٱللَّهُ يَٰعِيسَى ٱبْنَ مَرْيَمَ ءَأَنتَ قُلْتَ لِلنَّاسِ ٱتَّخِذُونِي وَأُمِّيَ إِلَٰهَيْنِ مِن دُونِ ٱللَّهِ قَالَ سُبْحَٰنَكَ مَا يَكُونُ لِي أَنْ أَقُولَ مَا لَيْسَ لِي بِحَقٍّ إِن كُنتُ قُلْتُهُ فَقَدْ عَلِمْتَهُ تَعْلَمُ مَا فِي نَفْسِي وَلَا أَعْلَمُ مَا فِي نَفْسِكَ إِنَّكَ أَنتَ عَلَّٰمُ ٱلْغُيُوبِ ﴿١١٦﴾ مَا قُلْتُ لَهُمْ إِلَّا مَا أَمَرْتَنِي بِهِ أَنْ﴾

اَعْبُدُواْ اللَّهَ رَبِّي وَرَبَّكُمْ وَكُنتُ عَلَيْهِمْ شَهِيدًا مَّا دُمْتُ فِيهِمْ

فَلَمَّا تَوَفَّيْتَنِي كُنتَ أَنتَ الرَّقِيبَ عَلَيْهِمْ وَأَنتَ عَلَى كُلِّ شَيْءٍ

شَهِيدٌ ۝ إِن تُعَذِّبْهُمْ فَإِنَّهُمْ عِبَادُكَ وَإِن تَغْفِرْ لَهُمْ فَإِنَّكَ

أَنتَ الْعَزِيزُ الْحَكِيمُ ۝ [المائدة: ١١٦-١١٨]

"And behold! Allah will say: 'O Jesus the son of Mary! Didst thou say unto men, worship me and my mother as gods in derogation of Allah?' He will say:' Glory to Thee! Never could I say what I had no right (to say). Had I said such a thing, Thou wouldst indeed have known it. Thou knowest what is in my heart, though I know not what is in Thine. For Thou knowest in full all that is hidden.' Never said I to them aught except what Thou didst command me to say, to wit, 'Worship Allah, my Lord and your Lord'; and I was a witness over them whilest I dwelt amongst them; when Thou didst take me up Thou wast the Watcher over them, and Thou art a witness to all things. If Thou dost punish them, they are Thy servants: if Thou dost forgive them, thou art the Exalted in power, The Wise. "

(Al Ma'idah: 116-118)

Allah says that on the Day of Judgment, He will ask Jesus in order to honor him and to reprimand those who ascribe false claims to him, namely that he is God, the son of God or His partner, far be He from all this. In turn, Jesus will answer Allah saying that He is far above having a partner and will show extreme politeness in addressing Allah. He will explain that it was Allah Who sent him and revealed the Holy Scripture unto him, will admit that Allah is his Creator and Provider of sustenance and will explain that Allah raised him unto Him when the Jews wanted to kill and crucify him, explaining how Allah saved him by rendering one of his disciples a lookalike of Jesus on whom they took their revenge. Next Jesus, by way of disowning the Christians, will tell Allah that if He wishes to torture them, they deserve it and if He wishes to forgive them, that will be entirely up to Him.

Imam Ahmad quotes Abu Dharr, may Allah be pleased with him, as stating that Allah's Messenger, peace and blessings be upon him , kept contemplating this particular verse all night long till the break of dawn, " *If Thou dost punish them, they are Thy servants: if Thou dost forgive them, thou art the Exalted in power, The Wise.* " (Al Maa'idah) He said,

$$\text{﴿إِن تُعَذِّبْهُمْ فَإِنَّهُمْ عِبَادُكَ وَإِن تَغْفِرْ لَهُمْ فَإِنَّكَ أَنتَ الْعَزِيزُ الْحَكِيمُ ﴿١١٨﴾} \quad \text{[المائدة: ١١٨]}$$

" *I asked Allah, Exalted be He, for intercession for my people and I was granted it, and it will be granted to whoever worships Allah solely with no partners.* "

(Al Maa'idah: 118)

Then Allah the Almighty says,

﴿لَّوْ أَرَادَ ٱللَّهُ أَن يَتَّخِذَ وَلَدًا لَّٱصْطَفَىٰ مِمَّا يَخْلُقُ مَا يَشَاءُ سُبْحَانَهُ هُوَ ٱللَّهُ ٱلْوَاحِدُ ٱلْقَهَّارُ ۝ خَلَقَ ٱلسَّمَوَاتِ وَٱلْأَرْضَ بِٱلْحَقِّ يُكَوِّرُ ٱلَّيْلَ عَلَى ٱلنَّهَارِ وَيُكَوِّرُ ٱلنَّهَارَ عَلَى ٱلَّيْلِ وَسَخَّرَ ٱلشَّمْسَ وَٱلْقَمَرَ كُلٌّ يَجْرِى لِأَجَلٍ مُّسَمًّى أَلَا هُوَ ٱلْعَزِيزُ ٱلْغَفَّارُ ۝﴾ [الزمر: ٤ - ٥]

" Had Allah wished to take to H imself a son, he could have chosen whom He pleased out of those whom He doth create: but Glory be to Him! (He is above such things.) He is Allah, The One, the Irresistible. He created the heavens and the earth in true (proportions): He makes the Night ove rlap the Day, and the Day overlap the Night: He has subjected the sun and the moon (to His law): each one follows a course for a time appointed. Is not He the Exalted in Power - He Who forgives again and again?"

(Al Zumar: 4-5)

Allah the Almighty says,

﴿سُبْحَانَ رَبِّ ٱلسَّمَوَاتِ وَٱلْأَرْضِ رَبِّ ٱلْعَرْشِ عَمَّا يَصِفُونَ ۝﴾ [الزخرف:٨٢]

"Glory to the Lord of the heavens and the earth, the Lord of the Throne (of Authority)! (He is free) from the things they attribute (to Him)!"

(Al Zukhruf: 82)

He also says, *"Say:*

$$﴿وَقُلِ ٱلْحَمْدُ لِلَّهِ ٱلَّذِى لَمْ يَتَّخِذْ وَلَدًا وَلَمْ يَكُن لَّهُ شَرِيكٌ فِى ٱلْمُلْكِ وَلَمْ يَكُن لَّهُ وَلِيٌّ مِّنَ ٱلذُّلِّ وَكَبِّرْهُ تَكْبِيرًا﴾$$

[الإسراء الآية ١١١]

'Praise be to Allah, Who begets no son, and has no partner in (His) dominion: nor (needs) He any to protect Him from humiliation: yea, magnify Him for His greatness and glory!"

(Al Israa':111)

Where Was Jesus Born?

Ibn Katheer states: As I have mentioned before, Jesus, peace be upon him, was born at Bethlehem, a town near Jerusalem." Ibn `Abbaas narrates: After Jesus had spoken in the cradle, he stopped speaking until he reached the natural age of speaking. Then Allah granted him wisdom and eloquence. However, the Jews, spoke a tremendous calumny against him and his mother. They used to call him "the son of the prostitute". In this respect, Allah the Almighty says,

60

$$\text{﴿وَبِكُفْرِهِمْ وَقَوْلِهِمْ عَلَى مَرْيَمَ بُهْتَنًا عَظِيمًا}$$

﴿١٥٧﴾ [النساء: ١٥٦]

"That they rejected Faith; that they uttered against Mary a grave false charge."

(Al Nisaa': 156)

When he was seven, his mother sent him to Al-Kuttaab[2]. Whenever the teacher tried to teach him a new thing, he found out that Jesus was aware of it. Upon noticing this, the teacher made him memorize Abu Jaad. But Jesus asked him, "What does Abu Jaad mean?" "I do not know", the teacher replied. Thereupon Jesus retorted, "How do you teach me something which you do not know?" The teacher next requested that Jesus teach him. Jesus sat in his teacher's place and said to him, "You can ask me". The teacher questioned him about the meaning of Abu Jaad. To the teacher's total amazement, Jesus replied, "The letter "A" refers to the bounties of Allah; "B" to the magnificence of Allah; and J to the beauty of Allah and His Pleasure."

It was a gift from Allah that Jesus showed miracles while he was young. When they heard about this, the Jews began to contrive conspiracies against him. As a result, his mother feared for his safety. Therefore, Allah inspired to her to escape with Jesus to a safe place. In this respect, Allah says,

$$\text{﴿وَجَعَلْنَا ٱبْنَ مَرْيَمَ وَأُمَّهُ ءَايَةً وَءَاوَيْنَـٰهُمَآ إِلَىٰ رَبْوَةٍ}$$

$$\text{ذَاتِ قَرَارٍ وَمَعِينٍ ﴿٥٠﴾}$$ [المؤمنون: ٥٠]

"And We made the son of Mary and his mother as a sign: We gave them both shelter on high ground affording rest and security and furnished with springs."

(Al Mu'minoon: 50)

Ibn Katheer states: "There is a difference of opinion among exegetes of the Qur'an as to the place of that high ground. The most correct opinion is that of Ibn `Abbaas. He states that the high ground refers to that river, concerning which Allah the Almighty says,

$$\text{﴿فَنَادَىٰهَا مِن تَحْتِهَآ أَلَّا تَحْزَنِى قَدْ جَعَلَ رَبُّكِ تَحْتَكِ سَرِيًّا﴾}$$

$$\text{﴿٢٤﴾}$$ [مريم : ٢٤]

"but (a voice) cried to her from beneath the (palm-tree):" Grieve not! "For thy Lord hath provided a rivulet beneath thee"

(Maryam: 24)

i.e., the place where Jesus was born was near Jerusalem.

When Were the Four Divine Scriptures Revealed?

Abu Zar'ah Ad-Dimashqi states: The Torah was revealed to Moses on the sixth night of Ramadaan; the Psalms was revealed to David on the twelfth night of Ramadaan, i.e., 482 years before the revelation of the Torah; the Gospel was revealed to Jesus, son of Mary, on the eighteenth night of Ramadaan, i.e., 1500 years after the revelation of the Psalms; and the Qur'an was revealed to Muhammad, peace be upon him, on the twenty-fourth night of Ramadaan. In his book of history, Ibn Jareer mentions that the Gospel was sent down to Jesus, peace be upon him, while he was thirty, and that he lived among his people until he was raised to heaven at the age of thirty-three.

Jesus Was Aided by Clear Signs:

Is-haaq Ibn Bishr states: When Jesus, son of Mary, peace be upon him, was sent as a Prophet for the Israelites and was supported by clear proofs, the Hypocrites and disbelievers among them started mocking and laugh-ing at him. They used to ask, "What did so-and-so eat yesterday? What did he store in his house?" As soon as he answered them, the believers' faith grew and increased whereas the hypocrites and disbelievers sank deeper in arrogance and disbelief.

Jesus had no house to seek refuge in. However, he used to wander and roam about from one place to another. The first time Jesus raised the dead was when he saw a woman sitting by a grave and weeping over her dead daughter. Upon seeing her, Jesus asked her, "What is the matter with you?" The woman replied, "My only daughter had died, and I vowed not to leave this place until I die or she is raised up again so that I can see her?" Jesus, then, said, "Will you return home, if you see her?" "Yes," answered the woman. Jesus went and performed two *Rak'ahs* (prayer units). He then sat beside the grave and cried, "O-calling the girl's name-! Get up by the will of Allah, the All-Merciful! "Thereupon the grave shook. Jesus cried for the second time and, by Allah's will, the grave cracked. Upon crying for the third time, the dead daughter came out of the grave shaking off the dust. Jesus, then, asked her, "What delayed you?" She replied, "At the first cry, Allah sent an angel to gather my organs; at the second, my life was brought back; and at the third,

I thought it was the Cry of Resurrection. As a result, my hair, eyebrows, and eyelashes turned gray out of fear of the Day of Judgement." The daughter turned to her mother and said, "O mother! Why did you cause me to experience the agony of death twice? O mother! Be patient and seek Allah's reward, as I have no desire to live longer." The daughter then said to Jesus, "O Allah's spirit and word! Ask Allah to take my life again and to relieve me of the agony of death." So Jesus prayed to his Lord and she was sent back to the grave. Upon learning of this, the Jews got so angry with him.

Ibn Katheer mentions that the Israelites asked Jesus, peace be upon him, to bring back to life Sam, the son of Noah. He prayed to Allah, Exalted be He, and He raised him up and then told them about the Ark. Then Jesus invoked Allah to cause him to die again, and it was done.

In *Surah* Al Maa'idah, Allah the Almighty and Most Truthful, says, *"Then will Allah say, "O Jesus, the son of Mary! Recount My favor to thee and to thy mother. Behold! I strengthened thee with the Holy Spirit so that thou didst speak to the people in childhood and in maturity. Behold! I taught thee the book and wisdom, the Law, and the Gospel."*

The Holy Spirit referred to in this verse is meant for Gabriel, peace be upon him; wisdom means writing and understanding; the Torah refers to the Divine Scripture revealed to Moses, the son of 'Imran, peace be upon him; and the Gospel stands for the Divine Scripture revealed to Jesus, the son of Mary, peace be upon him. Jesus, peace be upon him, memorized the Torah and the

Gospel.

Allah next says, *"And behold! Thou makest out of clay, as it were, the figure of a bird by My leave. And thou breathest into it and it becometh a bird by My leave."* That is to say Jesus managed, by Allah's leave, to shape clay into the form of birds and then breathed into it and it became a real bird. The phrase *"by My leave"* emphasizes the fact that he used to do those things only by the will and power of Allah.

Allah then says,

﴿إِذْ قَالَ ٱللَّهُ يَٰعِيسَى ٱبْنَ مَرْيَمَ ٱذْكُرْ نِعْمَتِى
عَلَيْكَ وَعَلَىٰ وَٰلِدَتِكَ إِذْ أَيَّدتُّكَ بِرُوحِ ٱلْقُدُسِ تُكَلِّمُ
ٱلنَّاسَ فِى ٱلْمَهْدِ وَكَهْلًا وَإِذْ عَلَّمْتُكَ ٱلْكِتَٰبَ
وَٱلْحِكْمَةَ وَٱلتَّوْرَىٰةَ وَٱلْإِنجِيلَ وَإِذْ تَخْلُقُ مِنَ ٱلطِّينِ
كَهَيْئَةِ ٱلطَّيْرِ بِإِذْنِى فَتَنفُخُ فِيهَا فَتَكُونُ طَيْرًۢا بِإِذْنِى
وَتُبْرِئُ ٱلْأَكْمَهَ وَٱلْأَبْرَصَ بِإِذْنِى وَإِذْ تُخْرِجُ ٱلْمَوْتَىٰ
بِإِذْنِى وَإِذْ كَفَفْتُ بَنِىٓ إِسْرَٰءِيلَ عَنكَ إِذْ
جِئْتَهُم بِٱلْبَيِّنَٰتِ فَقَالَ ٱلَّذِينَ كَفَرُوا۟ مِنْهُمْ إِنْ هَٰذَآ إِلَّا
سِحْرٌ مُّبِينٌ ﴿١١٠﴾ [المائدة: ١١٠]

"And thou healest those born blind and lepers by My leave. And behold! Thou bringest forth the dead by My leave. I did restrain the children of Israel from (violence to) thee when thou didst show them the Clear

Signs, and the unbelievers among them said,
'This is nothing but evident magic.' "

(Al Maa'idah: 110)

Allah restrained the children of Israel from doing harm to Jesus when they decided to crucify him. He raised him unto Himself and delivered him from them in order to protect him against harm and save him from death.

Allah the Almighty says,

﴿وَإِذْ أَوْحَيْتُ إِلَى ٱلْحَوَارِيِّنَ أَنْ ءَامِنُوا بِ
وَبِرَسُولِي قَالُوٓا ءَامَنَّا وَٱشْهَدْ بِأَنَّنَا مُسْلِمُونَ ﴿١١١﴾﴾

[المائدة: ١١١]

"And behold! I inspired the Disciples to have
faith in Me and Mine Messenger: they said,
'We have faith and do thou bear witness that
we bow to Allah as Muslims.' "

(Al Maa'idah: 111).

The inspiration referred to in the verse means that Allah guided them to faith, as He says, in another verse:

﴿وَأَوْحَىٰ رَبُّكَ إِلَى ٱلنَّحْلِ أَنِ ٱتَّخِذِى مِنَ ٱلْجِبَالِ بُيُوتًا
وَمِنَ ٱلشَّجَرِ وَمِمَّا يَعْرِشُونَ ﴿٦٨﴾﴾ [النحل: ٦٨]

"And thy Lord taught the Bee"

(Al-Nahl: 68)

$$﴿وَأَوْحَيْنَا إِلَى أُمِّ مُوسَى أَنْ أَرْضِعِيهِ فَإِذَا خِفْتِ عَلَيْهِ فَأَلْقِيهِ فِي الْيَمِّ وَلَا تَخَافِي وَلَا تَحْزَنِي إِنَّا رَادُّوهُ إِلَيْكِ وَجَاعِلُوهُ مِنَ الْمُرْسَلِينَ ٧﴾$$

[القصص: ٧]

"So We sent this inspiration to the mother of Moses: "Suckle (thy child), but when thou hast fears about him, cast him into the rive r"

(Al Qasas: 7)

Others interpret the word inspiration as referring to that kind of revelation via a Messenger and Allah's guidance to hearts to accept the truth, they say,

$$﴿وَإِذْ أَوْحَيْتُ إِلَى الْحَوَارِيِّنَ أَنْ ءَامِنُوا بِي وَبِرَسُولِي قَالُوا ءَامَنَّا وَاشْهَدْ بِأَنَّنَا مُسْلِمُونَ ١١١﴾$$

[المائدة: ١١١]

"We have faith and thou bear witness that we bow to Allah as Muslims"

(Al Maa'idah: 111).

Among the favors Allah bestowed on His bondman and Messenger Jesus, the son of Mary, was that He aided him with supporters and advocates so as to help him call people to solely worship Allah and not to ascribe associates with Him. This is similar to the aid Allah provided for His Messenger, Muhammad, peace and blessings be upon him, concerning which Allah says,

﴿وَإِن يُرِيدُوٓا۟ أَن يَخْدَعُوكَ فَإِنَّ حَسْبَكَ ٱللَّهُ هُوَ ٱلَّذِىٓ أَيَّدَكَ بِنَصْرِهِۦ وَبِٱلْمُؤْمِنِينَ ۝ وَأَلَّفَ بَيْنَ قُلُوبِهِمْ لَوْ أَنفَقْتَ مَا فِى ٱلْأَرْضِ جَمِيعًا مَّآ أَلَّفْتَ بَيْنَ قُلُوبِهِمْ وَلَٰكِنَّ ٱللَّهَ أَلَّفَ بَيْنَهُمْ إِنَّهُۥ عَزِيزٌ حَكِيمٌ ۝﴾ [الأنفال: ٦٢ ـ ٦٣]

"He it is that hath strengthened thee with His aid and with (the company of) the Believers; and (moreover) He hath put affection between there hearts: not if thou hadst spent all that is in the earth, couldst thou have produced that affection, but Allah hath done it: for He is Exalted in might, Wise".

(Al Anfaal: 62-63)

In *Surah* Ali 'Imraan, Allah the Almighty says,

﴿وَيُعَلِّمُهُ ٱلْكِتَٰبَ وَٱلْحِكْمَةَ وَٱلتَّوْرَىٰةَ وَٱلْإِنجِيلَ ۝ وَرَسُولًا إِلَىٰ بَنِىٓ إِسْرَٰٓءِيلَ أَنِّى قَدْ جِئْتُكُم بِـَٔايَةٍ مِّن رَّبِّكُمْ أَنِّىٓ أَخْلُقُ لَكُم مِّنَ ٱلطِّينِ كَهَيْـَٔةِ ٱلطَّيْرِ فَأَنفُخُ فِيهِ فَيَكُونُ طَيْرًا بِإِذْنِ ٱللَّهِ وَأُبْرِئُ ٱلْأَكْمَهَ وَٱلْأَبْرَصَ وَأُحْىِ ٱلْمَوْتَىٰ بِإِذْنِ ٱللَّهِ وَأُنَبِّئُكُم بِمَا تَأْكُلُونَ وَمَا تَدَّخِرُونَ فِى بُيُوتِكُمْ إِنَّ فِى ذَٰلِكَ لَءَايَةً لَّكُمْ إِن كُنتُم مُّؤْمِنِينَ ۝ وَمُصَدِّقًا لِّمَا بَيْنَ

69

يَدَىَّ مِنَ التَّوْرَىٰةِ وَلِأُحِلَّ لَكُم بَعْضَ ٱلَّذِى حُرِّمَ
عَلَيْكُمْ وَجِئْتُكُم بِـَٔايَةٍ مِّن رَّبِّكُمْ فَٱتَّقُوا ٱللَّهَ
وَأَطِيعُونِ ۝ إِنَّ ٱللَّهَ رَبِّى وَرَبُّكُمْ فَٱعْبُدُوهُ هَٰذَا
صِرَٰطٌ مُّسْتَقِيمٌ ۝ ﴿ [آل عمران: ٤٨ - ٥١]

"And Allah will teach him the book and Wisdom, the Law and the Gospel, and (appoint him) a Messenger to the Children of Israel, (with this message): 'I have come to you with a Sign from your Lord, in that I make for you out of clay, as it were, the figure of a bird and breathe into it, and it becomes a bird by Allah's leave: and I heal those born blind, and the lepers, and I quicken the dead by Allah's leave; and I declare to you what ye eat, and what ye store in your houses.' " That is to say Jesus could tell the people what they had eaten and what they stored for the coming days. *"Surely therein is a Sign for you"* i.e., a proof for the truth of my message. *"If ye did believe; (I have come to you) to attest the Law which was before me and to make lawful to you part of what was (before) forbidden to you."* This is an indication that Jesus, peace be upon him, abrogated some of the previous laws stipulated

by the Torah. *"I have come to you with a Sign from your Lord. So, fear Allah and obey me."*

(Ali 'Imraan: 48-51)

Scholars maintain that every Prophet performed, by Allah's leave, miracles that appealed to his own people. Here are some examples:

- Moses, peace be upon him, was sent at a time when magic was widespread and dominant. So Allah gave him a miracle that overwhelmed every magician. It was when the people made sure that it was but Allah's Supreme Power that they followed Moses and yielded to Allah.

- Likewise, Jesus, peace be upon, was sent at a time when doctors and physicians were most revered, and he performed a miracle that was totally inimitable. How extremely impossible was it for any doctor at the time of Jesus to heal those born blind and the lepers or to raise the dead!

- By the same token, Muhammad, peace and blessings be upon him, was sent to eloquent and fluent people. For this reason, Allah revealed to him the Glorious Qur'an which no falsehood can approach from before or behind, as it was sent down by the One Who is All-Wise, Worthy of all praise. Allah has defied the whole mankind and the Jinns to compose the like of the Qur'an or the like of ten *Surahs* or even one *Surah* of it, even if they are to back up one another with help and support. For it is the word of Allah, the Exalted and Glorified, Who has no comparison in being, attributes or actions.

$$\langle\!\langle\text{فَلَمَّا أَحَسَّ عِيسَى مِنْهُمُ الْكُفْرَ قَالَ مَنْ أَنصَارِيَ}$$
$$\text{إِلَى اللَّهِ قَالَ الْحَوَارِيُّونَ نَحْنُ أَنصَارُ اللَّهِ ءَامَنَّا بِاللَّهِ}$$
$$\text{وَاشْهَدْ بِأَنَّا مُسْلِمُونَ} \ ۝ \rangle\!\rangle \quad [\text{آل عمران}: ٥٢]$$

"When Jesus found unbelief on their part, he said, 'Who will be my helper to (the works of) Allah?' "

(Ali `Imraan: 52).

That is to say when the Israelites insisted on disbelief and arrogance, Jesus said, "Who will follow me in the way of Allah?" By *"helpers"*, Jesus meant the people who would help and support him to call people to the way of Allah, as it was the custom of Prophet Muhammad, peace and blessings be upon him, before the Hijra to address the pilgrims in the following manner: who will shelter me so that I can convey the message of my Lord, as Quraish has prevented me from doing so. This was his custom until he migrated to Madinah and Al-Ansaar gave him shelter, defended him, consoled and protected him against anyone who was to do him harm. By the same token, Jesus, the son of Mary, chose a company of the Israelites who believed in his message, helped and defended him, as well as followed the light which was sent down to him. In this respect, Allah says, *"Said, the Disciples, 'We are Allah's helpers: We believe in Allah, and do thou bear witness that we are Muslims. Our Lord! We believe in what Thou hast revealed and we follow the Messenger; then write us down among those who bear witness."* Ibn `Abbaas states: This is a reference to the nation of

Prophet Muhammad, peace and blessings be upon him. Ibn Katheer states: Disciples means supporters, as it is confirmed in the two *Sahihs* that when the Prophet, peace and blessings be upon him, wanted to delegate a person in the Battle of Al-Ahzaab (the confederates the trench), he delegated Az-Zubair Ibn Al-'Awaam. Then he wanted to delegate a person and he again delegated Az-Zubair, may Allah be pleased with him. The Prophet, peace and blessings be upon him, then commented: *"Every Prophet had a disciple, and Az-Zubair is my disciple."*

Allah the Almighty next says,

$$﴿وَمَكَرُواْ وَمَكَرَ ٱللَّهُ وَٱللَّهُ خَيْرُ ٱلْمَكِرِينَ﴾$$

[آل عمران: ٥٤]

"And (the unbelievers) plotted and planed and Allah too planed, and the best of planners is Allah."

(Ali `Imraan: 54)

It was narrated that when Jesus, peace be upon him, showed cogent proofs and crystal clear signs to the Israelites, most of them persisted in disbelief, arrogance, and errancy. They, moreover, plotted against him. They told the disbelieving king of that time that there was a man who led people astray, incited them to rebel against the king, and sowed the seeds of discord even between a father and his son, in addition to other false accusations. To make things worse, they claimed that he was a son of a prostitute, may Allah's curse be upon them. Enraged by their accusations, the king sent out some soldiers to detain and crucify Jesus. As soon as the soldiers surrounded

Jesus' house, they thought they were about to arrest him. However, Allah raised him up to Himself and saved him from their plot. Then Allah made one of those who were in his house look exactly like Jesus. Entering Jesus' house in the pitch of darkness, they thought that man was Jesus. They took him, tortured him, and put him to death on the cross. Then they stuck thorns in his head to demean him. This was Allah's plot to save His Messenger and raise him up to Himself leaving them under the illusion that they arrested Jesus. Allah, then, decreed that they would remain arrogant and ruthless forever, and suffer humiliation till the Day of Resurrection.

Allah the Almighty says,

﴿ وَإِذْ قَالَ عِيسَى ابْنُ مَرْيَمَ يَبَنِي إِسْرَءِيلَ إِنِّي رَسُولُ اللَّهِ إِلَيْكُم مُّصَدِّقًا لِّمَا بَيْنَ يَدَيَّ مِنَ التَّوْرَىٰةِ وَمُبَشِّرًا بِرَسُولٍ يَأْتِي مِن بَعْدِي اسْمُهُ أَحْمَدُ فَلَمَّا جَاءَهُم بِالْبَيِّنَٰتِ قَالُوا هَٰذَا سِحْرٌ مُّبِينٌ ۝ ﴾ [الصف: ٦]

"And remember, Jesus, the son of Mary, said, 'O Children of Israel! I am the Messenger of Allah (sent) to you confirming the law (which came) before me, and giving Glad Tidings of a Messenger to come after me, whose name shall be Ahmad.' But when he came to them with Clear Signs, they said, 'this is evident sorcery!' "

(Al Saff: 6)

The pronoun "he" may either refer to Jesus or to

Muhammad, peace be upon both of them. Allah also says,

﴿وَمَنْ أَظْلَمُ مِمَّنِ افْتَرَى عَلَى اللَّهِ الْكَذِبَ وَهُوَ يُدْعَى إِلَى الْإِسْلَامِ وَاللَّهُ لَا يَهْدِي الْقَوْمَ الظَّالِمِينَ ۝ يُرِيدُونَ لِيُطْفِئُوا نُورَ اللَّهِ بِأَفْوَاهِهِمْ وَاللَّهُ مُتِمُّ نُورِهِ وَلَوْ كَرِهَ الْكَافِرُونَ ۝﴾ [الصف: ٧ - ٨]

"Who doth greater wrong than one who invents falsehood against Allah, even as he is being invited to Islam? And Allah guides not those who do wrong. Their intention is to extinguish Allah' Light (by blowing) with their mouths: but Allah will complete (the revelation of) His Light, even though the unbelievers may detest (it)"

(Al Saff: 7-8)

Allah then urges the believers to defend Islam and support its Prophet saying,

﴿يَا أَيُّهَا الَّذِينَ آمَنُوا كُونُوا أَنصَارَ اللَّهِ كَمَا قَالَ عِيسَى ابْنُ مَرْيَمَ لِلْحَوَارِيِّينَ مَنْ أَنصَارِي إِلَى اللَّهِ قَالَ الْحَوَارِيُّونَ نَحْنُ أَنصَارُ اللَّهِ فَآمَنَت طَّائِفَةٌ مِّن بَنِي إِسْرَائِيلَ وَكَفَرَت طَّائِفَةٌ فَأَيَّدْنَا الَّذِينَ آمَنُوا عَلَى عَدُوِّهِمْ فَأَصْبَحُوا ظَاهِرِينَ ۝﴾

[الصف: ١٤]

"O ye who believe! Be ye helpers of Allah: as said, Jesus, the son of Mary, to the Disciples, 'Who will be my helpers to (the

work of) Allah?' Said the Disciples, "We are Allah's helpers!" Then a portion of the Children of Israel believed, and a portion disbelieved."

(Al Saff: 14)

The portion among the Israelites that disbelieved, denied Jesus' Prophethood, and falsely spoke against him and his mother a tremendous calumny were the Jews, may Allah's curse be upon them until the Day of Resurrection. Another group among Jesus' followers glorified him excessively; some called him the son of Allah; some claimed he is Allah; and yet some others claimed that Jesus is one of three gods which are united in the form of one God, i.e., the Father, the Son, and the Holy Spirit.

Allah next says,

﴿يَٰٓأَيُّهَا ٱلَّذِينَ ءَامَنُوا۟ كُونُوٓا۟ أَنصَارَ ٱللَّهِ كَمَا قَالَ عِيسَى ٱبْنُ مَرْيَمَ لِلْحَوَارِيِّنَ مَنْ أَنصَارِىٓ إِلَى ٱللَّهِ قَالَ ٱلْحَوَارِيُّونَ نَحْنُ أَنصَارُ ٱللَّهِ فَـَٔامَنَت طَّآئِفَةٌ مِّنۢ بَنِىٓ إِسْرَٰٓءِيلَ وَكَفَرَت طَّآئِفَةٌ فَأَيَّدْنَا ٱلَّذِينَ ءَامَنُوا۟ عَلَىٰ عَدُوِّهِمْ فَأَصْبَحُوا۟ ظَٰهِرِينَ ﴾ ﴿١٤﴾

[الصف: ١٤]

"But We gave power to those who believed against their enemies, and they became the ones that prevailed."

(Al Saff: 14).

That is to say Allah strengthened those who believed against their foes, and they became the uppermost.

﴿إِذْ قَالَ ٱللَّهُ يَٰعِيسَىٰ إِنِّي مُتَوَفِّيكَ وَرَافِعُكَ إِلَيَّ وَمُطَهِّرُكَ مِنَ ٱلَّذِينَ كَفَرُوا وَجَاعِلُ ٱلَّذِينَ ٱتَّبَعُوكَ فَوْقَ ٱلَّذِينَ كَفَرُوٓا إِلَىٰ يَوْمِ ٱلْقِيَٰمَةِ ثُمَّ إِلَيَّ مَرْجِعُكُمْ فَأَحْكُمُ بَيْنَكُمْ فِيمَا كُنتُمْ فِيهِ تَخْتَلِفُونَ ٥٥﴾ [آل عمران: ٥٥]

"O Jesus! I will take thee and raise thee to Myself and clear thee (of the falsehoods) of those who blaspheme; I will make those who follow thee superior to those who reject faith to the Day of Resurrection"

(Ali `Imraan: 55)

That is to say those who were close in following Jesus would be made superior to others. As Muslims believe that Jesus is Allah's bondman and Messenger -which is the most truthful belief - they were made superior to the Christians who went far in glorifying Jesus and placing him in a rank more than that which Allah bestowed on him. By the same token, the Christians were made superior to the Jews, since they were at least closer to Jesus' message than the Jews were.

Allah says,

﴿ٱلَّذِينَ يَتَّبِعُونَ ٱلرَّسُولَ ٱلنَّبِيَّ ٱلْأُمِّيَّ ٱلَّذِى يَجِدُونَهُ مَكْتُوبًا عِندَهُمْ فِي ٱلتَّوْرَىٰةِ وَٱلْإِنجِيلِ يَأْمُرُهُم بِٱلْمَعْرُوفِ وَيَنْهَىٰهُمْ عَنِ ٱلْمُنكَرِ وَيُحِلُّ

لَهُمُ ٱلطَّيِّبَٰتِ وَيُحَرِّمُ عَلَيْهِمُ ٱلْخَبَٰئِثَ وَيَضَعُ
عَنْهُمْ إِصْرَهُمْ وَٱلْأَغْلَٰلَ ٱلَّتِى كَانَتْ عَلَيْهِمْ ۚ
فَٱلَّذِينَ ءَامَنُوا۟ بِهِۦ وَعَزَّرُوهُ وَنَصَرُوهُ وَٱتَّبَعُوا۟
ٱلنُّورَ ٱلَّذِىٓ أُنزِلَ مَعَهُۥٓ ۙ أُو۟لَٰٓئِكَ هُمُ ٱلْمُفْلِحُونَ ﴿١٥٧﴾

[سورة الأعراف، الآية: ١٥٧]

"Those who follow the Messenger, the unlettered Prophet whom they find mentioned in their own (Scriptures), in the Law and the Gospel; for he commands them what is just and forbids them what is evil; he allows them as lawful what is good (and pure) and prohibits them from what is bad (and impure); he releases them from their heavy burdens and from the yokes that are upon them. So it is those who believe in him, honor him, help him, and follow the Light which is sent down with him, it is they who will prosper."

(Al A`raaf: 157)

Thus Jesus was the last Prophet sent to the Israelites. He gave them glad tidings about the seal of Prophets who would succeed him pointing out his name and attributes so that they might know him and follow his guidance.

The Story of the Table Spread

Allah Almighty says:

﴿إِذْ قَالَ ٱلْحَوَارِيُّونَ يَٰعِيسَى ٱبْنَ مَرْيَمَ هَلْ يَسْتَطِيعُ رَبُّكَ أَن يُنَزِّلَ عَلَيْنَا مَآئِدَةً مِّنَ ٱلسَّمَآءِ قَالَ ٱتَّقُوا۟ ٱللَّهَ إِن كُنتُم مُّؤْمِنِينَ ۝ قَالُوا۟ نُرِيدُ أَن نَّأْكُلَ مِنْهَا وَتَطْمَئِنَّ قُلُوبُنَا وَنَعْلَمَ أَن قَدْ صَدَقْتَنَا وَنَكُونَ عَلَيْهَا مِنَ ٱلشَّٰهِدِينَ ۝ قَالَ عِيسَى ٱبْنُ مَرْيَمَ ٱللَّهُمَّ رَبَّنَآ أَنزِلْ عَلَيْنَا مَآئِدَةً مِّنَ ٱلسَّمَآءِ تَكُونُ لَنَا عِيدًا لِّأَوَّلِنَا وَءَاخِرِنَا وَءَايَةً مِّنكَ وَٱرْزُقْنَا وَأَنتَ خَيْرُ ٱلرَّٰزِقِينَ ۝ قَالَ ٱللَّهُ إِنِّي مُنَزِّلُهَا عَلَيْكُمْ فَمَن يَكْفُرْ بَعْدُ مِنكُمْ فَإِنِّي أُعَذِّبُهُۥ عَذَابًا لَّآ أُعَذِّبُهُۥٓ أَحَدًا مِّنَ ٱلْعَٰلَمِينَ ۝﴾ [المائدة: ١١٢ - ١١٥]

"Behold! The Disciples said, 'O Jesus the son of Mary! Can thy Lord send down to us a Table set (with viands) from heaven?' Said Jesus, 'Fear Allah, if ye have faith.' They said, 'We only wish to eat there of and satisfy our hearts, and to know that thou hast indeed told us the truth; and that we ourselves may be witnesses to the miracle.' Said Jesus the son of Mary, 'O Allah our Lord! Send us

from heaven a Table set (with viands), that there may be for us- for the first and the last of us- a solemn festival and a Sign from Thee; and provide for our sustenance, for thou art the Best Sustainer (of our needs).' Allah said, 'I will send it down unto you: but if any of you after that resisteth faith, I will punish him with a penalty such as I have not inflicted on any one among all the peoples. "

(Al Maa'idah: 112-115)

Ibn Katheer states: Many stories has been narrated by Muslim early Muslims concerning the sending down of a table spread for the disciples of Jesus. It was reported that Jesus, peace be upon him, ordered the disciples to fast for thirty days. Upon completing the period, they requested him to ask his Lord to send down from heaven a table spread for them to eat of. Some of the early Muslims mention that they asked for a table spread because of their poverty and dire need. So they asked Jesus to pray to Allah so that He might send down for them a table spread to eat thereof and have energy and ability to continue their worship of Allah. Jesus, peace be upon him, said, *"Fear Allah, if ye have faith. "* He feared for them not to be grateful enough for such bliss. However, they insisted that he should ask his Lord for it. *" They said, 'We only wish to eat thereof' "* i.e., we are in a dire need of that food, *" and satisfy our hearts, "* if we see it coming down from heaven, *"and to know that thou hast indeed told us the truth"* i.e., our faith in you and your message will grow stronger, *"and that we ourselves may be witnesses to the miracle"* i. e., we will bear witness that it is a Sign from Allah and a cogent argument of your Prophethood and that you are telling the truth.

When the disciples insisted to have their wish fulfilled, Jesus, peace be upon him, went to his place of worship, closed his eyes and burst into tears. He then raised his hands to the sky and humbly prayed to Allah to answer his prayers and send down the table spread for his disciples. In this respect, Allah the Almighty says, *" Said Jesus the son of Mary," O Allah our Lord! Send us from heaven a table set (with viands), that there may be for us- for the first and the last of us – a solemn festival."* As- Soudey states: It means that we will make that day a feast to be glorified by us and those who will succeed us. It may also mean, as some state, that the table will be enough for our first and our last. *"And a Sign from thee."* Ibn Katheer explains: i.e., a clear proof of your power and might and of your answer to my prayers, so that they may believe in what I convey about You. *"And provide for our sustenance, for Thou art the Best Sustainer (of needs)"* meaning provide for us an easy food without discomfort or hardship. Allah then says, *"I will send it down unto you: But if any of you after that resisteth faith, I will punish him with a penalty such as I have not inflicted on any one among all the peoples"* i.e. in all times.

Allah then sent down a table spread from heaven and people watched it descending between two clouds. It kept on coming closer and closer, and as it was coming very close, Jesus, peace be upon him, prayed to his Lord so that it might be a mercy and not a wrath, a blessing as well as peace from Allah. The table kept on getting closer until it settled between Jesus' hands, peace be upon him, while covered with a napkin. Then Jesus, peace be upon him, uncovered it saying, " In the Name of Allah, the Best Sustainer." Upon uncovering it, people found seven whales, and seven loaves of bread. It was said that there was also some vinegar, pomegranate, and fruits. Jesus, peace be upon him, then ordered the disciples to eat of the table, but they said, " We will not eat until you eat (at first)." Thereupon Jesus said, " But you are the ones who asked for the table spread. Upon refusing to eat first, Jesus ordered the poor, the needy, and the sick to eat, so they ate, and every one with illness, sickness, or a handicap was cured instantly.

It was said that the table came down once a day, and people ate thereof, the first of them and the last of them, all amounting to about seven thousand persons. Then it used to come every other day, as it was the case with Salih's she-camel; people used to drink its milk day by day. Then Allah the Almighty ordered Jesus to make it exclusively for the poor and the needy and not the rich. This was annoying to lots of people, and hypocrites started talking about it, so it was completely raised up.

Scholars are in disagreement as to whether the table spread was sent down or not. Mujahid and Al-Hasan Al- Basri are reported to have stated that it did not come down, and that when it was said to them, *" But if any of you after that resisteth faith, I will punish him with a chastisement such as I have not inflicted on any one among all the people,"* They said, "We have no need for such a thing." Ibn Katheer states: This may find support in the idea that the event of the table spread is unknown to Christians and is not mentioned in their book, although scholars opine that it came down. Ibn Jareer states: Allah the Almighty has said, *" I will send it down unto you, "* and the promise of Allah is true. Ibn Katheer states: This opinion (i.e., the opinion of Ibn Jareer) is the most truthful, as it is confirmed by many narrations through the early Muslim. Allah knows best.

The Raising of Jesus to Heaven under Allah's Protection:

Allah the Almighty says,

﴿وَمَكَرُوا وَمَكَرَ اللَّهُ وَاللَّهُ خَيْرُ الْمَاكِرِينَ ۝ إِذْ قَالَ اللَّهُ يَٰعِيسَىٰ إِنِّي مُتَوَفِّيكَ وَرَافِعُكَ إِلَيَّ وَمُطَهِّرُكَ مِنَ الَّذِينَ كَفَرُوا وَجَاعِلُ الَّذِينَ اتَّبَعُوكَ فَوْقَ الَّذِينَ كَفَرُوا إِلَىٰ يَوْمِ الْقِيَٰمَةِ ثُمَّ إِلَيَّ مَرْجِعُكُمْ فَأَحْكُمُ بَيْنَكُمْ فِيمَا كُنتُمْ فِيهِ تَخْتَلِفُونَ ۝﴾

[آل عمران: ٥٤ - ٥٥]

"And (the Unbelievers) plotted and planned, and Allah too planned, and the best of planners is Allah. Behold! Allah said, 'O Jesus! I will take thee and raise thee to Myself and clear thee (of the falsehoods) of those who blaspheme, I will make those who follow thee superior to those who reject faith, to Day of Resurrection: then shall ye all return to Me and I will Jude between you of the matter where in ye dispute.' "

(Ali `Imraan: 54-55)

وَفِيمَا نَقْضِهِم مِّيثَٰقَهُمْ وَكُفْرِهِم بَِٔايَٰتِ ٱللَّهِ وَقَتْلِهِمُ ٱلْأَنۢبِيَآءَ بِغَيْرِ حَقٍّ وَقَوْلِهِمْ قُلُوبُنَا غُلْفٌۢ بَلْ طَبَعَ ٱللَّهُ عَلَيْهَا بِكُفْرِهِمْ فَلَا يُؤْمِنُونَ إِلَّا قَلِيلًا ۝١٥٥ وَبِكُفْرِهِمْ وَقَوْلِهِمْ عَلَىٰ مَرْيَمَ بُهْتَٰنًا عَظِيمًا ۝١٥٦ وَقَوْلِهِمْ إِنَّا قَتَلْنَا ٱلْمَسِيحَ عِيسَى ٱبْنَ مَرْيَمَ رَسُولَ ٱللَّهِ وَمَا قَتَلُوهُ وَمَا صَلَبُوهُ وَلَٰكِن شُبِّهَ لَهُمْ وَإِنَّ ٱلَّذِينَ ٱخْتَلَفُوا۟ فِيهِ لَفِى شَكٍّ مِّنْهُ مَا لَهُم بِهِۦ مِنْ عِلْمٍ إِلَّا ٱتِّبَاعَ ٱلظَّنِّ وَمَا قَتَلُوهُ يَقِينًۢا ۝١٥٧ بَل رَّفَعَهُ ٱللَّهُ إِلَيْهِ وَكَانَ ٱللَّهُ عَزِيزًا حَكِيمًا ۝١٥٨ وَإِن مِّنْ أَهْلِ ٱلْكِتَٰبِ إِلَّا لَيُؤْمِنَنَّ بِهِۦ قَبْلَ مَوْتِهِۦ وَيَوْمَ ٱلْقِيَٰمَةِ يَكُونُ عَلَيْهِمْ شَهِيدًا ۝١٥٩

[النساء: ١٥٥ ـ ١٥٩]

"(They have incurred divine displeasure): in that they broke their Covenant; that they rejected the Signs of Allah; that they slew the Messengers in defiance of right; that they said, 'Our hearts are the Wrappings.' Nay, Allah hath set the seal on the their hearts for their blasphemy, and little is it they believe; that they rejected Faith; that they uttered against Mary a grave false charge; that they said (in boast), 'We killed Christ Jesus the son of Mary, the Messenger of Allah'; but they killed him not, nor crucified him – but it *was made to appear to them and those who differ therein are full of doubts, with no (certain) knowledge, but only conjecture to follow, for of a surety they killed him not – Nay, Allah raised him up unto Himself; and Allah is Exalted in power , Wise; and there is none of the people of the Book but must believe in him before his death ; and on the Day of Judgment he will be a witness against them. "*

(Al Nisaa': 155-159)

Ibn Katheer states: Some of the major sins committed by the Jews for which they were cursed and dismissed out of Allah's mercy were: they broke their covenant and promises; they disbelieved in Allah's revelation and guidance as conveyed by His signs and miracles via the Prophets, peace be upon them, they dared to kill many of Allah's Messengers unjustly; they said, *"Our hearts are the Wrappings. "* Ibn `Abbaas and others explain: It means our hearts are blocked. Ibn Katheer expounds on this saying: It seemed as if they were searching for an excuse, namely that their hearts could not feel what He was saying. It was also said that they pretended that their hearts were the wrapping of knowledge because they had acquired enough of it. Allah the Almighty says, *" Nay, Allah hath set the seal on their hearts for their blasphemy, and little is it believe"* meaning their hearts got used to disbelief and oppression, *"that they rejected faith; that they uttered against Mary a grave false charge.* Ibn `Abbaas and others explain: They accused her of fornication, *"That they said (in boast)*, *We killed Jesus Christ, the son of Mary."* Ibn Katheer explains: It means we killed that one who pretended that he was Allah's Messenger. This is a form of irony and ridicule of them, just as the disbelievers said,

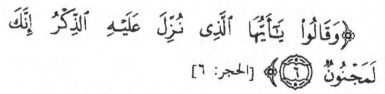

"O thou to whom the Message is begin revealed! Truly thou art mad (or possessed)!"
(Al Hijr: 6)

It was mentioned that when Allah sent Jesus, peace be upon him, with clear signs and evidence, the Jews, may Allah's curse, wrath, and punishment be upon them, envied him for whatever Allah had bestowed on him, namely Prophethood and clear miracles such as curing the blind, healing the leper, and bringing the dead back to life by Allah's permission. They denied his message and tried to harm him in the worst way they could until they forced him not to live amongst them, but to travel around with the company of his mother.

Moreover, they went to the King of Damascus at that time who was a disbeliever and a star worshipper. They told him about a man in Jerusalem who led people astray and perverted the king's subjects. Enraged by their news, the king wrote to his governor in Jerusalem to arrest Jesus, crucify him, and stick thorns on his head to stop him from harming people. The governor carried out the orders of the king, and headed with a group of Jews to the house of Jesus, peace be upon him, where they found him sitting with a group of his disciples. Their number is said to have been twelve, thirteen, or seventeen, and it was Friday afternoon.

Upon surrounding his house, Jesus felt their presence. As there was no way out, he said to his disciples, "Who amongst you will take my resemblance and be my companion in Paradise?" Thereupon a young man stood up, but Jesus thought he was too young. He repeated his question and the young boy stood up again. Jesus accepted him and Allah made him look exactly like Jesus. Then an opening in the ceiling was made to appear, and Jesus, peace be upon him, fell asleep and was raised up to heaven in such state. In this respect, Allah says,

﴿إِذْ قَالَ ٱللَّهُ يَـٰعِيسَىٰٓ إِنِّى مُتَوَفِّيكَ وَرَافِعُكَ إِلَىَّ وَمُطَهِّرُكَ مِنَ ٱلَّذِينَ كَفَرُوا وَجَاعِلُ ٱلَّذِينَ ٱتَّبَعُوكَ فَوْقَ ٱلَّذِينَ كَفَرُوٓا إِلَىٰ يَوْمِ ٱلْقِيَـٰمَةِ ثُمَّ إِلَىَّ مَرْجِعُكُمْ فَأَحْكُمُ بَيْنَكُمْ فِيمَا كُنتُمْ فِيهِ تَخْتَلِفُونَ ﴿٥٥﴾﴾ [آل عمران: ٥٥]

"O Jesus! I will take thee and raise thee unto Myself!"

(Ali `Imraan: 55)

His disciples went out of the house in the still of the night. When the Jews spotted this young man, they thought he was Jesus. They crucified him and stuck thorns in his hand to further humiliate him. People who crucified Jesus, peace be upon him, thought they killed him. Many sects of the Christians accepted their claims out of ignorance and insensibility, with the exception of those who were with Jesus inside the house, as they saw him raised up unto heaven. Allah has explained and clarified the whole story in the Glorious Qur'an which He revealed to his honorable Prophet whom He supported with miracles.

Allah the Almighty says,

﴿وَقَوْلِهِمْ إِنَّا قَتَلْنَا ٱلْمَسِيحَ عِيسَى ٱبْنَ مَرْيَمَ رَسُولَ ٱللَّهِ وَمَا قَتَلُوهُ وَمَا صَلَبُوهُ وَلَٰكِن شُبِّهَ لَهُمْ وَإِنَّ ٱلَّذِينَ ٱخْتَلَفُوا۟ فِيهِ لَفِى شَكٍّ مِّنْهُ مَا لَهُم بِهِۦ مِنْ عِلْمٍ إِلَّا ٱتِّبَاعَ ٱلظَّنِّ وَمَا قَتَلُوهُ يَقِينًۢا ۝ بَل رَّفَعَهُ ٱللَّهُ إِلَيْهِ وَكَانَ ٱللَّهُ عَزِيزًا حَكِيمًا ۝﴾ [النساء: ١٥٧ ـ ١٥٨]

"But they killed him not, nor crucified him, but so it was made to appear to them," i.e. they saw his lookalike and thought it was Jesus. *"And those who differ therein are full of doubts, with no (certain) knowledge, but only conjecture to follow,"* meaning those of the Jews who claimed to have killed him and those of the Christians who took this claim for granted are all in doubt and confusion. That is why Allah the Almighty says, *"For of a surety they killed him not -"* i.e. they were never certain that they had killed him. They always had their doubts. *"Nay, Allah raised him up unto Himself; and Allah is Exalted in Power,"* meaning He is not to be conquered, and He never lets down whoever seeks His

help. *"Wise"* *i.e.* Allah is Wise in all what He commands and decrees. He displays supreme sagacity, makes irrefutable arguments and enjoys great hegemony.

(Al Nisaa': 157-158)

It was reported that Ibn `Abbaas said: When Allah desired to raise his Prophet up unto heaven, Jesus walked up to his disciples with his head dripping wet. There were twelve disciples of his in the house. Then, he said, "Some of you will relinquish their faith in me twelve times after they had believed in me. Next he asked, who is willing to act as my lookalike, get killed instead of me and be with me in heaven? The youngest among them got up. Jesus said, sit. He repeated his question and the same young man got up anew, and answered, I am. Jesus said, you are the one. Then he became Jesus' lookalike, and Jesus was raised up from the house unto heaven. The Jews came asking for Jesus, found his lookalike, killed him then crucified him. Some of them lost their faith in him twelve times after they had believed in him. They were divided into three sects: one maintained that God remained among them for as long as He wished and was raised up to heaven. These are the Jacobites. Another sect believed that the son of God remained among them for as long as He wished and God raised him up unto Him. These are the Nestorians. The third stated that Allah's bondman and Messenger was among us for as long as He wished and Allah raised him up unto Him. These are the Muslims.

Sa'eed Ibn Al-Musayeb explains: When Jesus, peace be upon him, was crucified, he was thirty-three years of age. Ibn Katheer states: It was reported that people will be admitted to Paradise beardless, hairless, looking at their best and at the age of thirty-three. According to a different narration, as young as Jesus and as handsome as Joseph. It was mentioned that Ibn `Abbaas said: When Jesus was raised up unto heaven, a cloud approached him till it was close enough for him to sit on. Mary bid him goodbye in tears. Then she watched him being raised up unto heaven. Jesus threw her his garment saying, "This will be our sign till Judgment Day." He threw his hood on Sham`oon. His mother kept waving her hand to him till he totally disappeared. She loved him dearly, as she offered him the love of both parents, because he had no father, and she constantly kept him company.

Allah Almighty says,

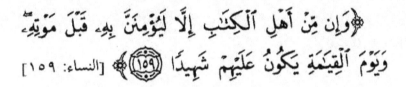

﴿وَإِن مِّنْ أَهْلِ ٱلْكِتَٰبِ إِلَّا لَيُؤْمِنَنَّ بِهِۦ قَبْلَ مَوْتِهِۦ وَيَوْمَ ٱلْقِيَٰمَةِ يَكُونُ عَلَيْهِمْ شَهِيدًا ۝﴾ [النساء: ١٥٩]

"And there is one of the People of the Book but must believe in him before his death."
(Al Nisaa': 159)

Al-Hasan, Qatadah and others explain: This means before the death of Jesus, peace be upon him. Allah has raised him up unto Himself and He will resurrect him before Judgment Day in such a manner that all believers and atheists will believe in him. Ibn Jareer explains: All People of the Book will believe in him before his death (i.e. before the death of Jesus).

Ibn Katheer states: This is the truth as will be illustrated shortly and it will be coupled with evidence. At the end of time and right before the Day of Judgment, Jesus will come down to earth, to kill the Dajjaal (Antichrist), kill the pigs, break the Cross, accept no Jizya from the People of the Book, accept either of the two choices; Islam or war, as was mentioned in a number of other *Hadiths*. Allah the Almighty says,

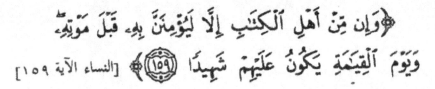

[النساء الآية ١٥٩] ﴿وَإِن مِّنْ أَهْلِ ٱلْكِتَٰبِ إِلَّا لَيُؤْمِنَنَّ بِهِۦ قَبْلَ مَوْتِهِۦ ۖ وَيَوْمَ ٱلْقِيَٰمَةِ يَكُونُ عَلَيْهِمْ شَهِيدًا ﴾

"And on the Day of Judgment he will be a witness against them."

(Al Nisaa': 159)

i.e. he will testify to all their actions which he bore witness to before being raised up to heaven and after his return to earth.

The Descent of Jesus before the End of the World

Al-Bukhari mentions on the authority of Abu Hurairah, may Allah be pleased with him, that the Prophet, peace and blessings be upon him, said, "By Him in Whose hand my soul is, the son of Mary will soon descend amongst you as a just judge. He will break the cross, kill pigs, and abolish the jizya, and wealth will pour forth to such an extent that no one will accept it, and one Sajdah (prostration in prayer) will be better than the world and what it contains."

Abu Hurairah used to say: You may recite the verse,

$$﴿وَإِن مِّنْ أَهْلِ ٱلْكِتَٰبِ إِلَّا لَيُؤْمِنَنَّ بِهِۦ قَبْلَ مَوْتِهِۦ وَيَوْمَ ٱلْقِيَٰمَةِ يَكُونُ عَلَيْهِمْ شَهِيدًا ﴾ (١٥٩)$$

[النساء الآية ١٥٩]

"Not one of the people of the book will fail to believe in him before his death and on the Day of Judgment he will be a witness against them."

(Al Nisaa': 159).

Ahmad reports on the authority of Abu Hurairah, may Allah be pleased with him, that the Prophet, peace be upon him, said,

"Jesus, the of Mary, will certainly pronounce Talbiyah for Hajj (Pilgrimage) or for 'Umra (Minor pilgrimage) or for

both in the valley of Rauhaa'." Ahmad also reports on the authority of Abu Hurairah, may Allah be pleased with him, that the Prophet, peace and blessings be upon him, said, *"The Prophets are paternal brothers; their mothers are different, but their religion is one. I am the nearest of all the people to Jesus, the son of Mary, as there has been no Prophet between us. He will descend to the earth, and if you see the following signs, know that he is Jesus: He is a ruddy man inclined to white; he will be dressed in red-colored clothes, his hair will be wet though water would not have touched it; he will break the cross, kill the pigs; abolish the Jizya; and call people to embrace Islam. In that time Allah will cause all religions to disappear except Islam; He will also kill the Dajjaal. Then the earth will become safe so that lions may graze with camels; tigers with cows, wolves with sheep; and so that children may play with snakes without being harmed. He will remain forty years, after which he will die and be prayed for by Muslims.*

Moslem states on the authority of Abu Hurairah, may Allah be pleased with him, that the Messenger of Allah, peace and blessings be upon him, said, *"The Last Hour would not come until the Romans would land at Al-'Amaaq or in Daabiq. An army consisting of the best (soldiers) of the people of the earth at that time will come from Medina (Madinah) (to counteract them). When they will arrange themselves in ranks, the Romans would say, " Do not stand between us and those (Muslims) who took prisoners from amongst us. Let us fight with them; and the Muslims would say, " Nay, by Allah, we would never get aside from you and from our brethren that you may fight them. They will then fight and a third (part) of the army would run away, whom Allah will never forgive. A third (part of the army), which would be constituted of excellent martyrs in Allah's sight, would be killed and the third who would never put to trial would win and they would be conquerors of Constantinople. And as they would be busy in distributing the spoils of war (amongst themselves) after hanging their swords by the olive trees, the Satan would cry: The Dajjal has taken your place among your family. They would then come out, but it would be of no avail. And when they would come to Syria, he would come out while they would be still preparing themselves for battle drawing up the ranks. Certainly, the time of prayer shall come and then Jesus, peace be upon him, the son of Mary would descend and would lead them in prayer. When the enemy of Allah would see him, it would (disappear) just as the salt dissolves itself in water and if he (Jesus) were not to confront them at all, even then it would dissolve completely, but Allah would kill them by his hand and he would show them their blood on his lance (the lance of Jesus Christ)."*

Landmark scholar Moslem reports on the authority of Abu Hurairah, may Allah be pleased with him, that the Prophet, peace and blessings be upon him, said, *"The last hour would not came unless the Muslims fought against the Jews and the Muslims would kill them until the Jews would hide themselves behind a store or a tree and a stone or a tree would say, 'Muslim, or bondman of Allah, there is a Jew behind me, come and kill him.' But the tree Gharqad would not say, for it is the tree of the Jews."*

Moslem also reported on the authority of An-Nawwaas Ibn Sam`aan who said, *"The Prophet, peace and blessings be upon him, made mention of the Dajjal one day in the morning. He sometimes described him to be insignificant and sometimes described (his turmoil) as very significant (and we felt) as if he were in the cluster of the date-palm trees. When we went to him (to the Holy Prophet) in the evening and he detected (the signs of fear) in our faces, he said, "What is the matter with you?" We said, " Allah's Messenger! You have made a mention of the Dajjal in the morning (sometimes describing him) to be insignificant and sometimes very important, until we began to think that might be present in some (near) part of the cluster of the date-palm trees. Thereupon he said, I harbor fear in regard to you in so many other things besides the Dajjal. If he comes forth while I am among you, I shall contend with him on your behalf, but if he comes forth while I am not amongst you, a man must contend on his own behalf and Allah would take care of very Muslim on my behalf (and safeguard) him against his evil. He (Dajjal) would be a young man with twisted, curly hair, and a one blind eye. I compare him to 'Abd-ul-Uzza Ibn Qataan. He who amongst you would survive to see him should recite before him the opening verses of Surah Al- Kahf. He would appear on the way between Syria and Iraq and would spread mischief right and left. "O bondman of Allah! I adhere (to the path of Truth)". We said, " Allah's Messenger! How long would he stay on earth? He said, "For forty days; one day is like a year and one day is like a month and one day like a week and the rest of the days would be like your days, We said, " Allah's Messenger! Would one day's prayer suffice for the prayers of a day equal to one year? Thereupon he said; "No, but you must make an estimate of time (and then* observe prayer)". We said: "Allah's Messenger, how fast would he walk upon the earth?" Thereupon he said: He would go fast as if he is driven by the wind. He would come to the people and invite them (to a wrong religion) and they would affirm their belief in him and respond to him. He would then give command to the sky and there would be rainfall upon the earth and it would grow corps. Then in the evening, their pasturing animals would come to them with high humps and full udders.

He would then come to another people and invite them. But they would reject him and he would go away from them and there would suffer drought and nothing would be left for them. He would then walk through the west, and say to it: Bring forth your treasures, and the treasures would come out and collect (themselves) before him like a swarm of bees. He would then call a person brimming with youth and strike him with the sword and cut him into two pieces and (make these pieces lie at a distance which is generally) between the archer and his target. He would then call (that young man) and he will come forward laughing with his face gleaming (with happiness) and it would be at this very time that Allah would send the Christ, son of Mary, and he will descend at the white minaret in the eastern side of Damascus wearing two garments lightly dyed with saffron and placing his hands on the wings of two angels. When he would lower his head, there would fall beads of perspiration from his head, and when he would raise it up, beads like pearls would scatter form it. Every non-believer who would smell the odor of his self would die and his breath would reach as far as he would be able to see. He would then search for him (Dajjal) until he would *catch hold of him at the gate of Ludd and would kill him. Then the people whom Allah had protected would come to Jesus, son of Mary, and he would wipe their faces and would inform them of these words: I have brought forth from amongst My bondmen such people against whom none would be able to fight; you take people safely to Tur, and then Allah would send Gog and Magog and they would swarm down from every slope. The first of them would pass the lake of Tiberias and drink out of it. And when the last of them would pass, he would say: There was once water there. Jesus and his companions would then be besieged here (at Tur, and they would be so much hard pressed) that the head of the ox would be dearer to them then one hundred dinars. Then Allah's Messenger, Jesus, and his companions would supplicate Allah who would send to them insects (which would attack their necks) and in the morning they would perish like one single person. Allah's Messenger, Jesus, and his companions would then come down to the earth and they would not find on the earth as much space as a single span which is not filled with their putrefaction and stench. Allah's Messenger, Jesus, and his companions would then again beseech Allah. Who would send birds whose necks would be like those of bactrin camels and they would carry them and throw them where Allah would will. Then Allah would send rain which no house of clay or (the tent of) camels' hairs would keep out and it would wash away the earth until it could appear to be a mirror. Then the earth would be told to bring forth its fruit and restore its blessing and, as a result thereof, there would grow (such a big) pomegranate that a group of persons would be able to eat, and seek shelter under its skin. A milch cow would* give so much milk that a whole party would be able to drink it. The milch camel would give such (a large quantity of) milk that the whole tribe would be able to drink out of that and the milch sheep would give so much milk that the whole family would be able to drink out of that. At that time Allah would send a pleasant wind which would soothe (people) even under armpits and would take the life of every Muslim and only the wicked would survive who would commit adultery like asses and the Last Hour would come to them."*

Imam Moslem narrated that a person came to `Abdulallaah Ibn `Amr Ibn Al-`Aas and said, "What is this *Hadith* that you narrated that the Last Hour would come at such and such time? Thereupon he said, "Glory be to Allah! There is no god but Allah. I decided that I would not narrate anything to anyone anymore. I only said that after some time you would witness an important event; the Sacred Mosque (Ka`bah), and so on...

He then reported that the Prophet, peace and blessings be upon him, said: *"The Dajjal would appear in my Ummah (nation) and he would stay (on earth) for forty – I can not say whether he meant forty days , forty months or forty years. And Allah would then send Jesus son of Mary who would resemble ' Urwa Ibn Mas`ood. He (Jesus the Christ) would chase him and kill him. Then people would live for seven years that there would be no rancor between two persons. Then Allah would send cold wind from the side of Syria that none would survive upon the earth having a speck of good in him or faith in him but he would die, so much so that even if some amongst you were to enter the innermost part of the mountain, this* wind would reach him even in that place and would cause his death. I heard Allah's Messenger (may peace be upon him) as saying, "Only the wicked people would survive and they would be as careless birds with the characteristics of beasts. They never appreciate the good nor condemn evil. Then Satan would come to them in human form and would say, 'Don't you respond?' And they would say, 'What do you want us to do?' He would command them then to worship the idols. Then the trumpet would be heard so loud that no one would hear it but he would bend his neck to one side and raise it from the other side. The first one to hear it would swoon and the other people would also swoon, then Allah would send or He would cause to send rain which would be like dew. The rain would cause the bodies of the people to grow. Then trumpets would be blown and they would stand up and begin to look (around). Afterwards it would be said, "O people, go to your Lord,

﴿وَقِفُوهُمْ إِنَّهُم مَّسْئُولُونَ ۝ ﴾ [الصافات الآية ٢٤]

"Make them stand there. And they would be questioned."

(Al Saaffaat: 24)

Then it would be said, "Bring out a group (out of them) for the Hell -Fire. Then it would be asked, "How much?" It would be said, "Nine hundred and ninety- nine out of every thousand for the Hell-Fire and that would be the day which would make the children get old because of its terror and that would be the day about which it has been said: "On the day when the shank would be uncovered".

Moslem reports on the authority of Hudhaifah Ibn Usaid Al-Ghifaari who said, *"The Prophet, peace and blessings be upon him, came to us all from 'Arafa as we were discussing the Last Hour. Thereupon he said, " It will not come until you see ten signs first: the raising of the sun from the west, the smoke, the beast, the people of Gog and Magog, the descent of Jesus, son of Mary, the Dajjal, and land—sliding in three places, one in the east, the other in the west, and the third in Arabia at the end of which fire would burn forth from Yemen, and would drive people to the place of their assembly."*

Ibn Katheer states: All these *Hadiths* are sound and authentic. They indicate that Jesus, peace be upon him, will descend to the earth, namely in Damascus at the eastern minaret on the time of dawn prayer. Ibn Katheer goes on to say that on the year 741AH a white minaret has been built on the Umayyad Mosque instead of that one which the Christians destroyed, and it is most likely that it is this minaret at which Jesus, peace be upon him, will descend. Upon his descent, Jesus will kill the pigs, break the Cross and abolish the Jizya, and will not accept any religion except Islam. Moreover, he will come out from the valley of Rauhaa' to pronounce Talbiya for *Hajj* or `*Umra* or for both of them. He will remain for forty years after which he will die and be buried with Prophet Muhammad, peace be upon him, and his two companions (Abu Bakr and `Umar).

Jesus: His Attributes and Virtues

Allah the Almighty says,

﴿مَّا ٱلْمَسِيحُ ٱبْنُ مَرْيَمَ إِلَّا رَسُولٌ قَدْ خَلَتْ مِن قَبْلِهِ ٱلرُّسُلُ وَأُمُّهُ صِدِّيقَةٌ كَانَا يَأْكُلَانِ ٱلطَّعَامَ ٱنظُرْ كَيْفَ نُبَيِّنُ لَهُمُ ٱلْآيَٰتِ ثُمَّ ٱنظُرْ أَنَّىٰ يُؤْفَكُونَ ٧٥﴾ [المائدة]

[الآية ٧٥]

"Christ the son of Mary was no more than a Messenger, many were the Messengers that passed away before him. His mother was a woman of truth."

(Al Maa'idah: 75)

Al-Bukhari and Moslem state in their two *Sahihs* (authentic books) that the Prophet, peace and blessings be upon him, said: *"If anyone bears witness that there is no god but Allah who has no associate, and that Muhammad is His bondman and Messenger, and that Jesus is Allah's bondman and Messenger, and His Word which He bestowed on Mary and a soul from Him, and that Paradise is true, and Hell is true, Allah will admit him into Paradise with the deeds which he has done even if those deeds were few."*

Al- Bukhari and Moslem also mention on the authority of Abu Mousa Al-Ash'ari that the Prophet, peace and blessings be upon him , said *"If a person teaches his slave girl good manners properly, educates her properly, and then manumits and marries her, he will get a double reward. And if a man believes in Jesus and then believes in me, he will get a double reward. And if a slave fears his Lord (i.e. Allah) and obeys his masters, he will too get a double reward."*

Moreover, Al-Bukhari reports on the authority of Ibn `Abbaas that the Prophet, peace and blessings be upon him, said, *"You will be resurrected (and assembled) barefoot, stark naked, and uncircumcised."* The Prophet then recited Allah's saying, **"As We began the fist creation, We shall repeat it: A promise We have under taken. Truly We shall do it."** He added," *The first to be dressed will be Abraham- then some of my companions will be taken to the right and to the left. I will say, "My companions! and it will be said," They had been converted since you left them," I will then say What the pious bondman Jesus, the son of Mary, said,*

﴿مَا قُلْتُ لَهُمْ إِلَّا مَا أَمَرْتَنِي بِهِ أَنِ اعْبُدُوا اللَّهَ رَبِّي وَرَبَّكُمْ وَكُنتُ عَلَيْهِمْ شَهِيدًا مَّا دُمْتُ فِيهِمْ فَلَمَّا تَوَفَّيْتَنِي كُنتَ أَنتَ الرَّقِيبَ عَلَيْهِمْ وَأَنتَ عَلَىٰ كُلِّ شَيْءٍ شَهِيدٌ ۝ إِن تُعَذِّبْهُمْ فَإِنَّهُمْ عِبَادُكَ وَإِن تَغْفِرْ لَهُمْ فَإِنَّكَ أَنتَ الْعَزِيزُ الْحَكِيمُ ۝﴾ [المائدة: ١١٧ - ١١٨]

"And I was a witness over them while I dwelt amongst them, when Thou didst take me up, Thou wast the Watcher over them, and Thou art a witness to all things. If Thou dost

punish them, they are Thy servants, and if
Thou dost forgive them, Thou art the Exalted
in power, the Al-Wise."

(Al Maa'idah: 117-118)

Furthermore, Al-Bukhari reports on the authority of Ibn `Abbaas that the latter said, "I heard Umar (i.e. Ibn Al-Khattaab), while addressing the people from the pulpit, saying, " I heard the Prophet, peace and blessings be upon him, say, *"Do not glorify me the same way the Christians glorified Jesus, the son of Mary, for I am but a bondman. So, call me Allah's bondman and Messenger."*

In addition to that, Al-Bukhari states on the authority of Abu Hurairah that the Prophet, peace and blessings be upon him, said: *"None spoke in the cradle but three (The first was), Jesus, (the second was) a man from the children of Israel called Juraij. While he was offering his prayers, his mother come and called him. He said (to himself), 'Shall I answer her or keep on praying?' (He went on praying and did not answer her). His mother said, 'O Allah! Do not let him die till he sees the faces of the prostitutes.' So, while he was in his hermitage, a lady came and sought to seduce him, but he turned her down. Therefore, she went to a shepherd and seduced him instead. As a result she gave birth to a child and claimed that it belonged to Juraij. Upon hearing her accusations, the people tore down his hermitage, drove him out and attacked him. Juraij performed the ablution and offered a prayer. Then he asked the child, 'O child! Who is your father?' The child answered, 'The shepherd.' After hearing this, the people said, 'We shall rebuild your hermitage of gold,' but he said, 'No, of nothing but mud,'*

(The third one to speak while still in the cradle was the hero of the following story). A lady from the children of Israel was nursing her child while a handsome rider passed by, She said, 'O Allah! Make my child like him.' On that the child left her breast, faced the rider and said, 'O Allah! Do not make me like him,' The child then started suckling her breast again, Abu Huraiah said, 'As if I were looking at the Prophet, peace and blessings be upon him sucking his finger (in way of demonstration.)' After a while a lady slave passed by them and she (i.e. the child's mother) said, 'O Allah! Do not make my child like this (slave girl).' On that the child left her breast and said, 'O Allah! Make me like her.' When she asked why, the child replied, 'The rider is one of the tyrants while this slave girl is falsely accused of theft and fornication.'

Al- Bukhari also reports on the authority of Salmaan that the period that was between the times of Jesus and Prophet Muhammad, peace and blessings be upon him, was six hundred years.

CPSIA information can be obtained
at www.ICGtesting.com
Printed in the USA
FSHW020530090320
67951FS